STEPPING OUT OF LINE

Believe in You

STEPPING OUT ^{OF} LINE

LESSONS FOR WOMEN WHO WANT IT THEIR WAY . . .
IN LIFE, IN LOVE, AND AT WORK

Nell Merlino

Broadway Books

New York

Published in the United States by Broadway Books, an imprint of
The Doubleday Publishing Group, a division of Random House,
Inc., New York.
www.broadwaybooks.com

BROADWAY BOOKS and its logo, a letter B bisected on the diagonal,
are trademarks of Random House, Inc.

Library of Congress Cataloging-in-Publication Data
Merlino, Nell.
Stepping out of line : lessons for women who want it their way . . .
in life, in love, and at work / Nell Merlino. — 1st ed.
p. cm.
1. Women—Psychology. 2. Self-esteem in women. 3. Self-
perception in women. 4. Self-acceptance in women. I. Title.
HQ1206.M44 2009
155.6'33—dc22
2008034707

ISBN 978-0-7679-2484-9

PRINTED IN THE UNITED STATES OF AMERICA

3 5 7 9 10 8 6 4 2

To my nieces, Allison, Maggie, and Helena

Contents

Acknowledgments / *ix*

Introduction / *1*

1 **STEPPING OUT WITH TAKE OUR DAUGHTERS TO WORK DAY** / *23*

2 **THE SYSTEM IS MORE MALLEABLE THAN YOU THINK** / *48*

3 **IMAGINATION IS ESSENTIAL** / *81*

4 **GAINING FROM COMPLAINING** / *135*

5 **WHAT IS HOLDING YOU BACK?** / *169*

6 **ACTIVATE WHO YOU KNOW** / *193*

7 **GIRLS LEARN EVERYTHING FROM WATCHING US** / *209*

Acknowledgments

Kath Delaney suggested that I write a book. We were standing in her kitchen, deep in Muir Woods outside of San Francisco, and I was in the early days of building Count Me In for Women's Economic Independence. I quickly dismissed the idea of a book, saying I didn't have time. (How often do we miss opportunities because we think we are too busy?) Kath and I had already been through so much together—three presidential campaigns, a huge Earth Day concert in Central Park, and my first silent meditation retreat. We had been to each other's weddings and knew each other's families. Despite my protests, she gave me the name of her friend, Linda Loewenthal, who was a literary agent in New York.

It took me months, but eventually I had coffee with Linda and she became my agent. I am so grateful to my dear friend Kath for seeing the book in me and for introducing me to Linda, who has been my guide through the book world.

Linda led me to Kris Puopolo, who has been my intelligent and supportive editor at Broadway Books. Thank you, Kris, for your excellent work, and to everyone at Broadway who has supported the book throughout this process.

I will never forget meeting Lindsey Pollak. She came right up to me as I entered an intimidating Working Woman conference at the height of the dot.com boom. She made me feel so welcome, helped me navigate the room, and followed up with me often. When it came time to find the writer to help me with my book, Lindsey was the first person I thought of and, after much trial and error, the only person I knew could complete my book with me. Lindsey, thank you for being so curious, brilliant, courageous, and committed to *Stepping Out of Line*.

"Believe in you" is a mantra at Count Me In. When you believe in you, your ambition, your accomplishments and your capabilities, others will too. Stepping Out of Line is something you do yourself, but none of us can accomplish very much all by ourselves. There are so many people who believe in me and to whom I am most grateful.

I am deeply grateful to:

My mother, Molly, and father, Joe, for living a life full of love, service, art, politics, and family. For loving me, teaching me, and encouraging me to Step Out of Line.

Carol Munter, for listening, challenging, and loving me no matter what.

Norman Levy and Tom Blatner, for knowing I would flourish as an entrepreneur.

Doug Gould, Tim Sweeney, Geoffrey Knox, and David

Eng, for allowing me to play a very small part in the fight against HIV and AIDS with the Gay Men's Health Crisis.

Kristen Golden, Miriam Zoll, Elliot Thomson, Therese Stanton, Marie Wilson, Idelisse Malave, Gloria Steinem, Janet Andre Block, Sarah Gould, Marlo Thomas, Jessye Norman, Helen Hunt, Jane Tollinger, Carol Jenkins, Betty Yee, Meredith Wagner and Ortho-Pharmaceutical (for giving us the seed money), and everyone else associated with the Ms. Foundation for Women and the successful launch of Take Our Daughters to Work Day, for your support and dedication.

The millions of girls, mothers, fathers, teachers, employers, reporters, producers, and editors who supported Take Our Daughters to Work Day, for helping to make girls more visible, valued, and heard.

Sharon Cohen, for asking Marie Wilson who it was that thought up Take Our Daughters to Work Day.

Stephanie Hanbury-Brown, for seeing the potential in Count Me In, for your strong board leadership and for your insistence that we get buttoned up and organized. Vickee Adams, Lorene Arey, Maureen Borzacchiello, Ned Cloonan, Shamaya Gilo, Deborah Kaye, Garnett Newcombe, Shelly Porges, Deborah Shah, Jed Scala, Peggy Wallace, and Vanessa Wilson, for serving on the Count Me In Board. Your time, wisdom, and guidance are essential.

Karen Scates, Beth Salerno, Terry Savage, Steve Alessio, Rich Tambor, and Richard D'Ambrosio of American Express, for helping me breathe life into the idea with your powerful belief in women entrepreneurs.

Susan Sobbott, Marcy Shinder, Michelle Dolberry, Lexi

Reese, Channing Barringer, and Anne Robinson, and the entire American Express OPEN team, for your insightful leadership, strategic investment and involvement in Make Mine a Million $ Business.

Ned Cloonan, Ed Lee, and James Chin for elevating our cause and clout, for your strategic investment, involvement, and global perspective.

Jean Hamerman, Claire Merlino, Amy Litt, Suzanne Michaud, JoAnn Gwynn, Helen Parker, Cori Viles, Simone Pero, Heather Kipnis, Isisara Bey, Tim Aston, and Stacey Straughter for working hard and smart to build Count Me In and our Make Mine a Million $ Business movement.

Hilary Blair, Margery Miller, Bill Dueease, Nely Galan, Valerie Morris, Simon Sinek, and Rosalyn Taylor O'Neil for bringing your best thinking, heart, and souls to our movement.

All of the Make Mine a Million $ Business awardees and finalists, for being the vanguard tidal wave of women entrepreneurs who will lead the country, community by community, to innovation, millions of new jobs and a stronger 21st century economy. Knockers Up!

Hillary Clinton, for your unwavering support of women and Count Me In. Any time I think about easing up on my mission, I think of you and just "keep going."

Suze Orman, for asking me how the book was coming along until it was finished, and for telling me when I was on the wrong track.

Beth Korein, my friend since 1980, for knowing me so well, reading every word in every draft of this book, asking thoughtful questions, making great suggestions, and always cheering me on.

Isisara Bey, my trusted colleague and longtime friend, for sharing and supporting my vision and for revealing yours in all its brilliance.

Lorene Arey, for being first in your appreciation, for being a bold, brilliant, and beautiful friend with your wit and wisdom. Long Live Lorene.

Edie Fraser, my friend, for inspiring me with your books and for being so generous with who and what you know.

Joe Merlino, my brother, for being a brilliant strategic colleague on the YWCA Week Without Violence, The Reebok Human Rights Awards, Count Me In and so much more.

Claire Merlino, my unflappable, observant, and precise sister, for your calm support and leadership at SCA Ltd. and Count Me In.

Kate Merlino, my sister, for being there for our mother and taking such good care of her so I can spend time writing, working, and not worrying.

Jim Merlino, my brother, for always reminding me that the Merlino family business is politics and that politics is ultimately about families.

Diane Wiesenberger and her partner Carole, for sending me on a blind date with Gary Conger, who is now my husband.

Gary Conger, my husband, my partner, my dearest friend, for keeping me current with your careful reading, cooking most of the meals and staying in with me on weekends while I worked on my book (our "study dates,"

with you painting and watching football while I wrote).
Thank you for never wavering in your love and patience.

Thank you all for believing in me.

Thank you all for inspiring me to Step Out of Line and
stay there.

STEPPING OUT OF LINE

Why Did I Write This Book?

Since I created Take Our Daughters to Work Day in 1992, thousands of women have asked me how I did it and how they, too, can make a difference in their own lives and in the world. My answer is always the same. You have to stop waiting for the world to change and decide that you will change it. You have to step out of line and live the life you want to live, create the work you want to do, and build the personal relationships that will make you happy. You—and all women—are capable of living the exact life you want. There is only one prerequisite: you must be willing to step out of line.

If you secretly know that you are capable of more than what you see around you, you are ready to step out of line. If you have a great idea for a new product or company or project, you are ready to step out of line. If you want to be a leader of your club or your school board or the country, you are ready to step out of line. If you want to change the terms of your relationships with the people in your life, you are ready to step out of line. If you are looking for an outlet for your bold, charismatic self and your secret imaginings, you are ready to step out of line.

This book will show you why stepping out of line is the key to getting whatever it is that you want—in life, in love, and at work. Here are your operating instructions:

How to Step Out of Line

1. Stop waiting for someone else—a partner, a parent, a boss, the government—to change your life and decide to actively pursue your biggest goals, dreams, ideas, and passions right now.

2. Repeat, as needed, in any area of your life.

Waiting in line is about conformity and order and following directions. It usually requires us to stand still and silent. It's about patiently waiting for our turn to talk, get a promotion, offer an opinion, or be next. Loyal soldiers march in line. Little children stand in line. Actors memorize a line in order to say the right thing. It's dangerous to "step over the line." We conform when we "toe the line." We are yelled at for being "out of line."

This book is about not waiting and stepping out of line instead. It requires a willingness to be seen and heard. To command attention. It will help you stop following other people and forge your own path, define your own terms, make your own rules, and trust your own instincts.

This may feel uncomfortable at first, and that is okay. But rest assured that stepping out of line does not have to mean turning your life upside down—it invites you to decide which lines you want to leave behind. You may want to step out of line to change your career while you feel perfectly fine with the status of your marriage. You may want to step out of line in your volunteer work while maintaining your current employment situation. Or, you may want to leap out of line, turn your current life upside down, and sign up for Doctors Without Borders (www.doctorswithoutborders.org). It's all up to you.

Not surprisingly, the idea for this book came to me while I was waiting in line—a line for the ladies' room. On this particular occasion, I found myself in a classic situation: you're on a long car ride, run into a rest stop to use the bathroom, and run smack into a long, long line.

On this occasion, my husband, Gary, and I were driving up the New York Thruway to his best friend's daughter's wedding in Vermont, in slow summer weekend traffic. After a few hours on the road, we parked in a massive rest stop parking lot and dashed inside. Together we pushed through two sets of glass doors. Gary went to the left, I went to the right and—*bam*, I hit it head on. The Line.

I had no choice but to join it and wait.

Most men must think that women take so long in the bathroom because we're fooling around, putting on lipstick, plucking stray hairs from our eyebrows, gossiping with other giggling gals. Believe me: if you've ever been in a ladies' room at a rest stop on the New York Thruway, you want to get in and out of there as quickly as possible. We take so long because we're waiting in line.

While I stood in the rest stop ladies' room line, irritated and uncomfortable and trying to be patient, I started to wonder what other women do when they wait—how they feel, what they think about, what attitudes they have about always waiting in these lines. Do they resent it? Do they wish it could be different?

At some point I noticed a woman a few places in front of me. She kept turning around and looking at the men's room—and the lack of a line to enter it. She kept looking at the men's room, then looking to the front of our line to see how much more time she had to wait, and then looking to the back of our line to see how much longer the line had become. She kept looking back and looking forward, and she didn't appear happy to be waiting. She was physically playing out what was going on in my head.

I saw that woman's actions as symbolic of where women find ourselves today: looking back at how far we've come since our great-grandmothers' times, looking forward to how far we still can go to achieve the lives we want for ourselves and our daughters, and glancing over at the guys for comparison or reference.

Although I had planned to drive the next stretch of our trip, I asked Gary to drive instead so I could start writing about all the thoughts I'd had in line. From the moment I watched that other woman waiting, my mind was off and

running. I had to get it all down, so I took out my Black-
Berry and started tapping:

> what are we waiting 4?
> how many hrs of our lives do women spend waiting in
>   line?
> why not do something about it?
> what else do we wait 4?
> think about women & girls with no bathrooms who wait
>   in endless lines for everything
> what can we do?

I couldn't get the topic out of my head. It struck me
that the ladies' room line is an excellent metaphor for the
state of women today. Think about it: You walk into most
airports, movie theaters, malls, or highway rest stops and
there appear to be equal facilities for men and women.
There's the same sign, same tiles, same products, and numbers of stalls and sinks. But, when you look at the situation more closely, things are not equal. There is almost
always a line for the ladies' room and rarely, if ever (unless
you're at a sporting event where beer is being consumed),
do you see a line for the men's room.

It is curious that we tolerate this. Women have already
eliminated so many other lines in our modern lives—with
Botox in our foreheads and Spanx on our rear ends—and
cut down waiting time using technologies like FreshDirect,
EZ Pass, airline e-tickets, Moviefone.com, and FastPass
lines at Disney World. Why don't we use our power, our
brains, and our pocketbooks to eliminate lines to board

rooms, political back rooms, and ladies' rooms? Whatever the potential solution, why don't we step out of these long lines and do something about these—and other situations—that continue to slow us down and hold us back?

I say choose to defy the odds, to not only survive but to thrive in the face of challenges from economic disasters, glass ceilings, aging, and injustice. History and the recent past tell us to step out of line—step out of the usual places we are expected to be, for that is where real progress and power live.

My mother, Molly McGoogan, made ceramic parts for fighter planes at a Lenox China factory where she had been making figurines, and Barack Obama's grandmother assembled B-29's at Boeing. Both were among 20 million women who answered Rosie the Riveter's call to step out of their homes, and they saved the American economy during World War II. Women went to work in factories in unprecedented numbers, helped the war effort, and then went back home as soon as the men returned from the war, not returning to the workforce in such large numbers until the 1970s. In her concession speech after the 2008 presidential primary, Hillary Clinton talked proudly about the 18 million cracks she and the people who voted for her had put in the glass ceiling, knowing that someday soon it will be completely shattered. And while most swimmers end their careers at twenty-five, in 2008 Olympian Dara Torres, at age forty-one, set an audacious goal to win an individual gold medal. She missed winning the individual gold by a fraction of a second, but went on to win individual silver and bronze medals and has become an iconic inspiration for women and athletes everywhere.

This highly public, "one step forward, two steps back" of women's progress reminds me of a similar moment in the early 1990s, when Anita Hill testified about the sexual harassment she experienced while working for Clarence Thomas, an event that provoked a valuable discussion of women and the workplace. Ultimately, the Senate Judiciary Committee did not believe Anita Hill, but because of her testimony, women around the country knew that sexual harassment was not something they had to tolerate.

Soon after Anita Hill's famous testimony, the Ms. Foundation for Women (www.ms.foundation.org) hired me to create a campaign to address the problem of falling self-esteem in adolescent girls. People were starting to wonder if the women's movement had failed the next generation of women. My response was to create a campaign, Take Our Daughters to Work Day, that helped girls be more visible, valued, and heard. That day made people see girls and women differently ever after.

As you will see in the coming chapters, you can use many of the lessons I learned planning Take Our Daughters to Work Day to live the life you want. This book is filled with stories from my own life and stories from a wide variety of women who took the actions necessary to live life on their terms. These stories will inspire you to step out of line whether you're single, married, lesbian, young, old, retired, wealthy, in debt, living on a farm, running a company, and/or working as a full-time mom. This book will inspire you to lead your life in a way that speeds the pace of progress for you and all women and increases your satisfaction in life, in love, and at work. It will offer suggestions and strategies for improving your relationship with money, finding a life partner, taking political action, and more. It will inspire you to go back to school, date online, adopt a child, make time for a hobby, launch your own blog, secure flextime at work, grow an organic garden, become more physically active, or do anything else you've been waiting, wishing, or hoping to do.

About Me

Who am I to write this book and guide you through a world where women step out of line, stand out, and live life on their terms? We've done this sort of thing together before. You may be familiar with my work creating Take Our Daughters to Work Day for the Ms. Foundation or the not-for-profit organization I founded, Count Me In for Women's Economic Independence (www.countmein.org). Or you may know about our Make Mine a Million $ Business® program (www.makemineamillion.org). We've stepped out of line with Make Mine a Million $ Business, inspiring one million women entrepreneurs to step out of their comfort zone and reach $1 million or more in revenues. It will be a historic achievement (only 243,000 of the 10.5 million U.S. women business owners are at $1 million in revenue now) that will create a minimum of four

million new jobs and pump $1 trillion into the U.S. econ-
omy.

I also helped produce the Twentieth Anniversary Earth
Day Concert in 1990, which was attended by close to one
million people in Central Park (www.earthday.net); with
my brother Joe I created the YWCA Week Without Violence, which ran for over five years around the country; I
did advance work on Nelson Mandela's first trip to New
York after he was released from prison and on dozens of
presidential campaign events for Walter Mondale, Mike
Dukakis, and a few for Bill Clinton; I organized the distri-
bution of 100,000 condoms on the streets of New York
with the Gay Men's Health Crisis; and was the communications director for the NGO Forum on Women in Beijing, the largest international gathering of women ever
held, with over 40,000 women in attendance and 5,000
reporters. Some people have called me a professional
rabble-rouser with a very active imagination.

My parents are responsible for my big-picture thinking,
creativity, and social conscience. Joe and Molly Merlino
were active citizens in Trenton, New Jersey (www.trentonnj.
com), where I grew up. My dad was a lawyer and New Jersey state senator and my mother was, and still is, a wonderful painter and community activist.

I was chubby from the age of nine and generally known
as "outspoken" (if you liked that sort of thing) or "bossy" (if
you didn't). When I was eleven, my favorite aunt, Connie,
a former showgirl in Las Vegas, offered to buy me a whole
new wardrobe if I lost thirty pounds.

I never got that new wardrobe from my aunt.

However, as a 2007 article in my hometown paper, the *Trenton Times* declared, I did grow up to become "Trenton's most accomplished homegrown feminist," "forceful and bombastic," "armed with contagious enthusiasm . . . [and] impassioned social awareness," and "[exhibiting my] mother's beguiling charm."

Phew!

How did I get to this point as an adult? Chubby and bossy and the daughter of political activists who took me along to voter registration drives, I figured out pretty early on that I wasn't going to grow up to be Doris Day. Most girls feel this way at a certain point—that they're not pretty or cute enough—but too many women keep hoping for, or relying on, being pretty or sexy or thin enough. I guess when even the promise of a new wardrobe didn't work for me, I started to focus on other things. Like arguing about politics with the nuns at the Blessed Sacrament School and wearing my father's World War II fatigue jacket over my school uniform.

I had to laugh when that same *Trenton Times* article proclaimed, "No one was surprised when, at 21, Nell Merlino took a job as a union organizer." After that, I worked on various political campaigns and eventually started my own strategic communications business—entrepreneurship is always a good option for a "bossy" girl.

With this book, I'm marshalling all of the experience I've gained and the lessons I've learned myself and from the people I've met to help women like you to step out of line, stand out, and make your life fit your wildest dreams.

Why Step Out of Line

One of the most famous lines of women is the Rockettes, the high-kicking precision dancers who perform at Radio City Music Hall in New York. I once read a newspaper story about how new dancers were selected to be in the line. The dancer had to be a very specific height, shape, and weight to be chosen—and, until 1987—the women were all Caucasian. Management thought a darker-skinned person would disrupt the symmetry of the line. "One or two black girls in the line would definitely distract. You would lose the whole look of precision, which is the hallmark of the Rockettes," said their director at the time, Violet Holmes. According to Bruce Lambert in a *New York Times* article, "Rockettes and Race," they wouldn't even allow the white Rockettes to have suntans. That is the kind of line we are all stepping out of—the lines that demand that we conform or else be excluded, ignored, inauthentic, or invisible.

Envision the freedom and power of stepping out of that line. Think of all the possibilities it opens up. Stepping out of line means using your imagination to determine the exact life you want, even if that life looks nothing like the life of anyone else. It means changing the systems that can feel so immovable—such as family, work, power, politics, and success—to fit your personal definitions of those terms. Finally, stepping out of line means being for you: knowing that you are fully responsible for yourself—your safety, your happiness, your success.

Stepping out of line is absolutely not about navel-gazing. It's about getting comfortable with what you want and what your values are, and then working to see your vision reflected in the world. This does not mean that you can't be for other people, too. In fact, as you'll see in many of the stories throughout this book, being for other people is incredibly important to achieving your own goals. Stepping out of line does, however, mean that you are for yourself first, and you know that your safety, balance, and success are yours to create and control. This is a message you've heard before, that counterintuitive instruction we get on airplanes: to put your own oxygen mask on first before placing it on the child sitting next to you.

Put Your Oxygen Mask on First and Keep Breathing

In order to help and support your family, your community, your company, or the world, you must take care of yourself first.

Stepping Out of Line on the Runway

Kate Hanni stepped out of line.

You may never have heard of her, but you probably recall the uproar in late 2006 and early 2007 because passengers on several domestic flights sat waiting on runways for six hours or more, with overflowing toilets and no access to water. One of those passengers was a forty-seven-year-old real estate agent named Kate Hanni, who was stuck aboard an American Airlines jet with her husband and two children. Kate, who told reporters she had never written a letter of complaint in her life, decided then and there that she would fight for legislation to make lengthy confinement on an airplane illegal. Instead of doing what everyone did—feeling frustrated and upset and then doing nothing when the ordeal was over—Kate took action.

She started meeting with her local congressman, commenting on Internet bulletin boards, enlisting volunteers to help her effort, and collecting videos from stranded passengers to post on YouTube.com. By September 2007, when she was featured in an article on the front page of the business section of the *New York Times,* Kate had gathered 18,000 signatures for an online petition supporting her passengers' bill of rights.

Kate Hanni stopped waiting for someone else and started taking action herself about an issue that affected her family and many other people. But there's more to Kate's story. At the time of her airplane runway saga, Kate's career as a successful real estate agent had been on hold because of a 2006 incident in which a man lured her to a vacant home on the pretense of being a potential home buyer. He attacked her and threatened her life. She resisted, and thankfully he ran away. After that experience, Kate could not stand to be alone and stopped going out to sell real estate. She spent months afterward in post-traumatic stress therapy.

During the weeks and months of organizing on behalf of her passengers' bill of rights, however, Kate felt an internal shift. Her fears of being alone dissipated. "I stopped all the therapy," she told Jeff Bailey from the *Times* in his article "An Air Travel Activist Is Born." "This has taken over my life. It helped me overcome those fears," Kate said.

Stepping out of line and taking action on behalf of yourself and others—as Kate Hanni did after her ordeal on the airport runway—can change a system that affects millions of people. But Kate's story shows how it works the other way, too. When Kate spoke up and took action to change the system, she began to overcome her personal fears. This can happen when you step out of line, too.

Stepping Out of Line to Save Thousands of Lives

Jody Williams stepped out of line and into the public eye by creating the International Campaign to Ban Landmines (ICBL, www.icbl.com) and subsequently won the Nobel Peace Prize for her work. Knowing that hundreds of thousands of people have been killed or maimed by landmines over the past decades, and that 15,000 to 20,000 new casualties are caused by landmines each year, Williams began a movement to eradicate all antipersonnel landmines around the world. Thanks to Williams and her team at ICBL, a network of more than 1,400 groups in over 90 countries is now working locally, nationally, and internationally to remove all current landmines and ban all future landmines forever.

What enabled Williams to accomplish in six years what dozens of powerful organizations, including the United Nations, had been unable to do in dozens of years?

"I have a deaf schizophrenic brother who people were mean to when I was young," she told the *Independent* of London. "I couldn't understand why people would be mean to him because he was deaf. That translated into wanting to stop bullies being mean to . . . people, just because they are weak."

And how did her world-altering project begin?

"When we began, we were just three people sitting in a room . . . It's breathtaking what you can do when you set a goal and put all your energy into it," she told the *Christian Science Monitor*. "I think you have to believe you're right. You say, 'This is what we're going to achieve, and this is how we're going to do it.' And if people get upset about it, tough."

That's all it takes to begin to live the life you want, and to live in the kind of world that you want. When you decide "this is what I believe and what I am going to achieve," there is no limit to what you can accomplish. Think about every woman who's ever competed in a beauty contest. Practically every contestant tells the host that if she gets the crown she wants to help poor children or promote world peace. What if all the women saying this—and all the people watching—stopped wishing and took action immediately, like Jody Williams did? The message of this book is to take your dreams seriously. Nothing is holding you back from pursuing them.

Stepping Out of Line for Love

Like Kate Hanni and Jody Williams, we all have the power to change systems large and small. But every act of stepping out of line doesn't have to include a national movement. You can step out of line in very personal ways, like the way you seek and find a significant other.

I certainly didn't follow the "traditional" path to love and marriage. Around the time I was turning forty, I sat in a meeting with my accountant going over my taxes. After reviewing my numbers and complimenting me on the growth of my business, she asked if I was seeing anybody. When I said no, she suggested I go on a blind date with a man who was the older brother of a client of hers. "He's a great guy and he's in the right tax bracket!" she told me. This was a few years after *Newsweek* came out with a cover story saying that a single forty-year-old woman had a better chance of being killed by a terrorist than getting married. Lucky for me, that guy, Gary Conger, and I hit it off, dated, moved in together, and squeaked in just past the deadline, getting married when I was forty-one. I'll share much more about our story in future chapters.

My story looks practically old-fashioned when compared with the way people are now meeting and mating. Today, single people of any age who want to be in a relationship don't have to wait or give up or even hope for a setup. According to an article on MSN.com, over 40 million Americans (a full 40 percent of the U.S. single population) use online dating services to meet people. More than 120,000 marriages a year occur as a result, says *On-*

line Dating magazine. Now women can simply type our preferences into an online dating search engine and . . . voila! Dozens of available faces appear, with facts about their education, occupation, family background, religion, love of dogs, fear of snakes, and pretty much anything else you'd want to know.

Millions of online daters have ditched the system of waiting to find a partner through parents, yenta relatives, sorority sisters, debutante balls, or even the local bartender. By making a change in their behavior—stopping the wait for Prince or Princess Charming, stepping out of line, and starting a keyword search on exactly what they desire in a partner—hundreds of thousands of women are finding the exact relationships they want.

Stepping Out of Line to Pump

Another deeply ingrained "line" in our society is the belief that a mother's place is at home. Lodged among the endless debates about whether new moms should go back to work, when they should go back, and what happens when they do is the issue of how working mothers handle the physical realities of having a new baby and a job. I'm talking about the most longstanding of women's traditions: breast-feeding.

If you're a working mom with an infant, you may be spending long hours hunched uncomfortably in a bathroom stall, pumping breast milk for your baby. For the past twenty-five years, Patricia Kelly has made a career of helping women in this situation. She has built a business as a consultant to corporations on the creation of lactation rooms for working moms. Pat is well aware that breastfeeding and pumping are not always welcome in public, especially in the most traditionally masculine of places: a corporate office. She's spent her career working to change that.

Pat convinces companies to make women feel welcome as both productive employees and nurturing moms. With close to 70 percent of women with children in the workforce, and a substantial proportion of those breast-feeding at any given time, she has put the issue of lactation rooms and technology on the radar screens of employers large and small. In the process, Pat and her daughter, Joan Ortiz, now a partner in her company, Limerick, Inc. (www.limerick inc.com), found out that women also needed pumps that were fast, easy, safe, and comfortable. Instead of waiting for someone else to create a better pump, Pat and Joan took advantage of cutting-edge technology and designed what women wanted. Their PJ's Comfort hospital-grade electric breast pump is a state-of-the-art pump that—by the way—is the first FDA–approved advancement in breast pump technology in fifteen years!

My guess is that many working moms had feelings of guilt about going back to the office and felt that the time, discomfort, and annoyance of pumping was the price they had to pay. It isn't. A better way was possible. The world has changed to make women more visible in the workplace, and technology has developed to help make time-saving products possible. Pat and Joan understood this, and they started to figure out what it would take to make women's lives better. At the same time, they helped create a community for the current and future women who want to breast-feed at work. Who knows what new advances in lactation will take place now that Pat and Joan have stepped out of line and gotten things rolling?

A History of Stepping Out of Line

Kate Hanni, Jody Williams, Pat Kelly, Joan Ortiz, and millions of women seeking companions online are examples of the amazing things that happen when women take responsibility, step out of line, and live life on their terms. The system begins to catch up with them and people start to change their view of what women can do.

There is plenty of historical precedent for women stepping out of line. Our grandmothers and great-grandmothers eliminated much disrespect and waiting from our lives by winning the right to vote, own property, receive equal pay, and obtain credit in our own names. Enough women have walked through enough doors for the first time repeatedly now, that we are tolerated, accepted, and in some cases welcomed into almost every sector of society. The growing numbers of women who work in positions of influence and power present new opportunities for women to stop waiting in every area of our lives.

We are at an important time in women's history. Growing up I watched *Queen for a Day,* where homemakers won washing machines and Mixmasters, and now I have the privilege to run the Make Mine a Million $ Business program, where women business owners compete for the opportunity to win an award package of financing, laptops, phone systems, routers, and professional coaching. Today, women are running news organizations, federal agencies, emergency rooms, police departments, 10.5 million American businesses, the House of Representatives, and a growing number of countries in addition to managing their families.

And yet, we still have far to go. Hecklers demand that a female U.S. senator running for president "iron my shirt," and news organizations revel in misogyny. We still represent a paltry percentage of U.S. Congress and a handful of state governors and corporate CEOs. Most media images continue to celebrate women primarily for thinness and beauty.

But things are changing all the time. Lactation rooms and breast pumps, for example, would not have been as valued thirty years ago when fewer women were working and nursing at the same time. We don't even know yet what needs women will have thirty years from now. The world evolves and women's needs evolve. The opportunities are so exciting. Stepping out of line opens us up to create better family dynamics, innovative products and companies, new politics, and more responsive infrastructures. All we need to do is activate our imaginations, stay focused, and step up on behalf of our goals and dreams.

You Have Everything You Need

I promise you that stepping out of line will affect what you do with your time, knowledge, hard-earned money, personal connections, and the resources at your fingertips. The stories and lessons in this book will prove that when you stop waiting, you can achieve more than you've ever imagined. You will gain insights and confidence in yourself and your choices, because you will see how to progress from imagining something to making it happen. You'll learn whom to call, where to find resources, how many people it takes to pull it off, how it feels, why it succeeds, and why it fails. You will experience what it's like to make a difference at home, at work, or in the world, rather than waiting and hoping for something to happen.

That day while I waited at the New York Thruway rest stop, I imagined a ladies' room with enough room for all. I later learned that I wasn't alone in my imaginings. Neither are you. You don't have to reinvent the wheel if you, too, want something more out of life. There are proven steps and lessons for knowing what change to make and how to go about making it. This book will help guide you as you dare to imagine your life your way and take action to make it happen.

By the end of this book, you'll believe that anything can change. We'll talk about stepping out of line in every place women feel stuck, unwelcome, or ignored—waiting until we feel smart enough to start a business, hoping for that phone call from him or her, debating whether to run for office, or procrastinating about saving until we have enough money. A key message of this book is that women are "enough" already. We have everything we need: the brains, bodies, spirit, and boldness to step out of line. The less time we spend following others, the more time we can spend enjoying our loved ones, making money, making friends, learning, and—in my vision—making the entire world a more welcoming place for women and girls. Just imagine what will happen when women put ourselves first, seize the day, and get comfortable with our power. Everyone will benefit. Join me in Stepping Out of Line and together all of our power, ability, confidence, and compassion will be revealed.

1

STEPPING OUT WITH TAKE OUR
DAUGHTERS TO WORK DAY

A phone call woke me up the morning after the very first Take Our Daughters to Work Day in April 1993. It was Wyatt Andrews, an old-school, serious, senior correspondent for *CBS Evening News*, calling from one of those phones that was embedded in the backs of airplane seats before they had tiny TVs with forty-seven channels. He was on the "power plane," the shuttle between Washington, D.C., and New York, with all the businesspeople in power suits drinking power coffee and reading their morning newspapers.

Wyatt told me he was calling because while he was walking down the aisle of that plane, he had seen Take Our Daughters to Work Day stories and photos on the front page of everyone's papers: *USA Today*, the *New York Times*, *The Washington Post*, *New York Daily News*, the *Wall Street Journal*, and others. There were photos of girls in every conceivable profession, dressed in uniforms ranging from hard hats to chef's toques to surgical masks to dainty pearls. There were girls in goggles soldering circuit boards. Girls reading fetal heart monitor graphs. Girls flying flight simulators. Girls walking through the halls of Congress. Girls computing. Girls lunching. Girls meeting. Girls everywhere.

"You did it," he said over and over. "You did it! You did it!"

Weeks earlier, Wyatt had interviewed me in New York for a national story. He had asked me tough questions, like whether the need for Take Our Daughters to Work Day was an indictment of the women's movement, if it was an indication of the failure of people like Gloria Steinem and others to change the world for women. I had said no, it was absolutely not an indication of failure. In fact, it was a mark of our success so far and a recognition of just how long it takes to make lasting, systemic, social and economic change.

During this celebratory phone call, Wyatt also mentioned to me that he had become an overnight sensation at his two daughters' school, because of his story on Take Our Daughters to Work Day. He was not famous because he was a newscaster. He was famous because everyone at school wanted to find out more about Take Our Daughters to Work Day. They had seen his news story and lined up to ask him whether they were planning the day correctly for their daughters. Wyatt said he'd never had so much interest in a single story. Everyone wanted to talk about and be part of Take Our Daughters to Work Day.

"You did it," he kept saying on the phone that morning. "You did it!"

The Steps to Change

Much of what I know about making change I learned or confirmed in the process of making my vision of Take Our Daughters to Work Day come to life. The story of this event—which changed my life as well as the lives of millions of girls—highlights many of the themes we will explore in this chapter and later chapters:

- Start with the end in mind. Define what success looks like and feels like to you. Define the desired impact of your actions.
- Activate your imagination. Whatever you are struggling with in your life, envision the best outcomes you possibly can. You have to see it before you can devise a plan to get there. Imagine how other people feel or how they might approach the challenge.
- Expect and listen to resistance to your idea or plan. Other people's criticism and questions help you find out what people are afraid of, what they are protecting. When used constructively, resistance is valuable information.
- Inspire, activate, and mobilize who you know. Engage all the help you need. Drop any notion that you have to—or can do—anything significant alone.
- Expand your definition of success to include others. As you step out of line, you will likely find that other people will follow your lead.

- Write it all down. None of the inspiring messages and stories in this book replaces the need for a strong plan. Take it from a communications expert: a strategic outline and a few clearly written paragraphs can go a long way.

As you will see from the Take Our Daughters to Work Day story, creating change is not magic. It happens by putting one foot in front of the other and using every bit of creativity, information, and support you can gather. A written plan is also essential. It doesn't have to be fancy, but it needs to be your road map that reminds you of what you are doing and why. Like everything else you want to succeed at, making change requires commitment, focus, and discipline. And to begin with, it takes imagination.

The Story of Take Our Daughters to Work Day

One of the most frequent questions people ask me is how I came up with the idea for Take Our Daughters to Work Day. The short answer is that I used my imagination. The longer answer is that I wanted other girls to have the kind of experience that I had going to work with my parents.

The Take Our Daughters to Work Day story begins in 1992, when Carol Gilligan completed a study that documented a pattern of strong, vital girls devolving into tentative, unsure young women as they passed through adolescence. Gilligan found that most girls' confidence levels plummeted by the time they reached their teens. By high school, more than two-thirds of girls had lost their self-confidence and faced poor self-image and low expectations. This meant eating disorders in girls as young as age eleven; a doubling of the incidence of depression for late adolescent girls as compared to boys; at least one suicide attempt for over 20 percent of teenage girls; and over a million pregnancies for those between the ages of twelve and nineteen.

The Ms. Foundation for Women wanted to launch a big effort to do something about this. I'd caught the foundation's attention because of a campaign I had helped organize with the Gay Men's Health Crisis to publicize the tenth year of the AIDS epidemic. The Ms. Foundation decided to hire me to come up with a campaign to make adults aware of the tragic loss of self-esteem that girls experience in adolescence. I knew this required a big idea, a way for girls to be valued for their ideas, strength, and aspirations and not just their cuteness.

Around this time I attended a retirement dinner for my father. I sat there looking around at all of the people my father had worked with over the course of his public service career, and thought about how my meeting all these people and observing them at work had influenced my own choices in life. I had gone to the office and on the campaign trail with my father and often observed him working. I had also seen my mother raising five children and painting on canvas, theater scenery, and public murals. I had gone to my mother's art studio and observed her and the other five women painters with whom she rented the space. I knew what my parents did for a living and I learned from watching them that they loved their work.

During the retirement dinner, I started to see a video unreeling in my mind's eye of a crowded New York City subway filled with girls traveling with their parents or other adults to work. There were as many girls as adults on this train. What if for one day, everyone focused on the potential of young women? What would that look like? For a national campaign to get attention, I knew that girls had to appear someplace that people never imagined girls being. Girls would need to step out of school for one day and populate workplaces across the nation and around the world.

Immediately, I started to imagine physically how such a thing would occur, and what help we would need to make my vision a reality. And I began to write down a plan. Take Our Daughters to Work Day was born. I started with a vision of the way things could be, and then step by step I worked to bring that vision to life. You can do this, too.

Start with the End in Mind

Write down or cut out pictures of what you ultimately see for yourself and others in life, love, and work. The more specific you can be, the more likely you will be able to communicate your vision to others so they can help you get there.

As you become clearer on your image of what you want in your life, you also need to define the finish line: What will be your evidence that this success has occurred? Defining success is a process of determining what's important to you and then setting clear outcomes to know you've accomplished your goals. In the case of Take Our Daughters to Work Day, our vision was a world where girls are visible, valued, and heard. Our definition of success was a day where as many girls as possible went to work with somebody. We measured the ultimate success of the first Take Our Daughters to Work Day in news clippings and letters by the pound, letters from girls and poll numbers that said over 2 million had participated in the first day. Girls' images were everywhere and they were being taken seriously. In the years since, over 100 million people have participated!

Can your definition of success change over time? Absolutely. You complete certain goals and set others. You might go down one path and decide that it's not really what you want. Circumstances change and your goals can change with them. Think about all the women who leave the corporate workforce because "success" in that realm turns out not to be satisfying to them. There is satisfaction in success. If you don't feel satisfied when you reach your goal, then it's probably time to rethink your definition.

**Set Specific, Time-Sensitive Goals; Write Them Down
and Post Them Where You Can See Them**

Further hone your unique definition of success by determining the actual numbers, dates, dollar amounts, or other specific markers you
want to achieve. This way, you'll be able to mark incremental successes
and celebrate when you've reached your ultimate goal. Vague goals
produce vague results.

Getting Started

Looking back, it's almost hard to imagine a time before
Take Our Daughters to Work Day. It's become a per-
manent part of our culture, appearing in the scripts of
popular TV shows—such as *ER, The Simpsons,* and *The
Office*—and the frames of comic strips like Garry Trudeau's
Doonesbury.

But in 1993, when we were planning the event from my
home office in New York City, we weren't sure how it
would all turn out. After the big vision, the detail work begins. There's no magic to this part of the process. Once we
had our overarching definition of success for Take Our
Daughters to Work Day, we proceeded to the rather mun-
dane but crucial next step: we wrote up a one-pager. That's
it. Nothing fancy. Just a simple Word document with a description of why we were doing this, when it would occur,
and who it would help and inspire—parents, daughters,
employers, and teachers.

To bring you into the detail work, picture this scene: we had three people at my office and three full-time staffers at the Ms. Foundation, all working long days and nights to plan and promote the day. This was pre-Internet, so everything was done by phone, mail, fax, and in-person meetings. There was no e-mail blasting, online researching, blogging, text messaging, or video conference calling. Phones were ringing off the hook and letters were streaming in from parents, teachers, business owners, and girls from across the country.

We received hundreds upon hundreds of faxes a day on those old fax machines with the rolls of slick paper. Eventually we were receiving so many faxes in giant swirls of white, shiny paper that they overtook the fax room and we had to find a volunteer just to cut all the paper as it spewed out of the machines! One of the biggest purchases we made the first year was a plain paper fax machine. The Ms. Foundation's fax machine got so clogged that they started sending people to my personal fax number.

Facing Resistance

It is hard to imagine now, but there were people who did not believe an event like Take Our Daughters to Work Day could or should happen. In fact, in my initial meetings there was resistance and fear about the notion of adults bringing girls into the workplace.

There were concerns about insurance, safety, legality,

and disruption of work. There were questions about whether one single day would really make a difference in girls' lives. Would girls be better off if we gave them each the money for therapy? (Seriously, that was one suggestion.) Some board members and advisors were concerned that girls would take one look at women in administrative positions and get discouraged about their career prospects. Others cynically voiced concerns that prostitutes might bring their daughters to work.

At one meeting, a member of the Ms. Foundation raised her concern that if girls spent the day at Lincoln Center with Jessye Norman, the successful opera singer and Ms. Foundation board member, they would think success meant being the one "star" and life would ultimately disappoint most of them. Jessye had the best response. She said, "If what girls love is singing and theater, I will expose them to the entire staff of Lincoln Center and they'll learn about thousands of jobs related to opera, not just the job of the lead singer." She believed, as do I, that girls are smart enough to understand the range of opportunities available to them.

We also had to do some work convincing teachers. Around that time, the American Association of University Women (www.aauw.org) had made videos for teachers to show them—to their absolute shock and amazement—that they called on more boys than girls in class, even when equal numbers of boys and girls raised their hands. We started sharing this research and showing these videos and received lots of media coverage on the topic. You can tell people something is happening, but until they see it, they're often not convinced.

And then there was the talk about the boys. Would boys feel left out and lose their self-esteem because there is a day just for girls? Wasn't this reverse discrimination? In fact, the first fax I received on the first Take Our Daughters to Work Day was from the American Men's Association, demanding that we include boys. I called the man who sent the fax and offered to send him all of our material so they could create a day for boys. They never did.

Name an argument against Take Our Daughters to Work Day and I've heard it. There has been resistance from day one. If you're wondering about my answers to the above concerns about prostitutes and opera singers, well, first of all, I've always argued that we need to resist the old-fashioned notion that we have to "protect" girls and women from reality. We need to replace illusions with reality. We need to engage them and say, "Anything you see, even though you may not see yourself in that position, is something you can do or not do. You have a choice." I wanted girls to understand that if you choose something, then you figure out what you have to do to get there. As for the boys, from the very beginning we spoke about the curriculum we created for them. Boys would spend Take Our Daughters to Work Day learning about inequality and why girls needed a special day. We would show boys how women had been discriminated against and what an important element of society their female classmates are.

As for the fear of prostitutes taking their daughters to

work, suffice it to say that girls whose mothers are prostitutes know what their moms do already. Exposing those girls to other kinds of work is especially critical.

Expect and Listen to Resistance

Whenever you try to change and grow, you will undoubtedly experience resistance, fear, and criticism from other people and from yourself. Anticipate this, listen to the concerns, and have a strategy to incorporate the valid ones into your plans.

Listening

There was no map to follow for Take Our Daughters to Work Day, so I started asking a lot of questions and then got a lot of people to help me make it happen. That's how you start any big project: by stumbling around, reading a lot, and putting it all together.

One of the ways we anticipated and eliminated much of the resistance to Take Our Daughters to Work Day was by talking to as many people as possible and gathering information. As the resistance was coming in one ear, in the other we were getting strong indications from teachers, school administrators, parents, and others that Take Our Daughters to Work Day was not only necessary, but also had the potential for enormous success.

Talking to people who worked with girls every day made all the difference. In 1992, we began our efforts to convince the mayor of New York City to invite all 250,000 city employees to participate in the first Take Our Daughters to Work Day the following year. We knew we needed the endorsement of educators to smooth the way with parents, teachers, and employers who were concerned about the negative impact of girls missing one day of classroom instruction, as well as a myriad of other possible problems.

We arranged to meet informally with a group of junior high school principals to discuss the merits and logistics of our program. After some spirited discussion, a woman named Patricia Black, principal of Martin Luther King Junior High School, who was clearly the "dean" of the principals, told me and the group an incredible story.

As a good and seasoned junior high school principal, Pat had relationships with large corporations in New York City who were often looking for students to fill internships and summer jobs. Given that the overwhelming majority of New York City public school students quality for the free school lunch program, paid employment and internships were critical to helping students generate income and see a different future.

Pat knew an executive woman who was looking for a student with exceptional computer skills to intern with her that summer. Pat knew this was an extraordinary opportunity and she knew just the right girl to send for the interview. She called Maria, a thirteen-year-old star computer class student, into her office and told her about the opportunity. She gave Maria the corporate woman's name and an address in Midtown Manhattan and told her that the appointment was set for 2 p.m. the following Tuesday.

Tuesday at 2 p.m. came and went and Pat got a call from her executive friend at the corporation. Maria hadn't shown up for the scheduled appointment. The executive suggested that maybe Pat had been wrong in her judgment that Maria was the perfect candidate for the position. Pat didn't think that was the problem and called Maria into her office. It was then she learned that Maria had never before been out of the Bronx. Maria said she had gotten on the wrong subway and never made it to Midtown.

Pat called the corporate executive back, explained the challenge, set another appointment, and helped Maria to carefully plan out a travel route on a subway map. To everyone's surprise and frustration, Maria missed the second appointment. A very frustrated Pat called Maria into her office again and asked why she had missed the appointment. "I know you can do this work and it's a great opportunity," Pat told her.

Sobbing, Maria explained that she had arrived at the Midtown office building with its huge revolving doors, marble and chrome entrance, security turnstiles and cameras, and she just couldn't get up the courage to walk through and find her way upstairs in the giant tower. She had never seen anything like it before and had also never imagined herself in a place like that. Her mother, aunts, and grandmothers did not work outside the home or venture far from the neighborhood.

So, once again Pat called her corporate contact, explained the situation, and begged for one more appointment. This time she said that she would personally travel with Maria to the interview. Happily, together with her trusted principal, Maria made it to the third interview and was able to walk into a world that she had never seen, had never even imagined. She got that internship and went on to work during school vacations all through high school, attended City College, and became a sought-after management information systems specialist.

After listening to Pat's story, there wasn't a principal in the room who didn't have a similar story about the importance of girls seeing new opportunities and experiencing them. From that point forward, I knew Take Our Daughters to Work Day was viable.

Get More Opinions than Your Own

Confidence is a huge asset, but it doesn't replace the need to test your ideas and plans with other people. There is great value in seeking advice from people with more experience, less experience, different backgrounds, and various dispositions. Trust your instincts and do some market research.

Say It Loud

My knowledge that we would be successful grew deeper when *Parade* magazine ran a story about Take Our Daugh-

ters to Work Day in May 1992. It became clear that girls
and parents from across the country and all walks of life
identified with the concept.

How did we get that story in *Parade?* I had thought
about the media angle early in my imaginings, knowing
from my political background that press coverage is essential for a large public campaign. In early 1992 I had done
the first one-page description of Take Your Daughter to
Work Day. That April, I was sitting in the conference room
of the Ms. Foundation with Kristen Golden, the project
director, when Gloria Steinem walked in. I had never
really spoken with her before. She was wearing a red pash-
mina shawl and leopard-print miniskirt. She walked in
and said, "What are you doing?" Kristen introduced me
and pushed our one-page write-up to Gloria. Gloria read
it, picked up a pen, crossed out "Your" and wrote "Our."
She then took the piece of paper, folded it up, and put it in
the pocket of her skirt. She said, "I'm going to lunch with
Walter Anderson [then publisher of *Parade*]. If he asks me
what's new, I'll give him this."

Sure enough, he did ask her and she gave him that
piece of paper. A month later, an article appeared. *Parade*
wrote a few paragraphs about Take Our Daughters to
Work Day and included a picture of Gloria.

From that article we received close to ten thousand letters! One letter in that huge wave of mail was postmarked
Philadelphia. A group of homeless mothers wrote to the
Ms. Foundation asking them to please find some people
with jobs to take their daughters to work. They explained
that they wanted their daughters to see and experience a

different life than the one they were able to show them now. And some people were worried what poor women's and prostitutes' daughters would do?

In the early months of 1993, momentum kept building and we began to receive more mainstream media attention and endorsements. Gloria Steinem and I attended a lunch with the editors of the major women's magazines and they all committed to putting moms and daughters on their covers to promote the program. Anna Quindlen wrote an op-ed piece about us for the *New York Times,* titled "Take Her With You." And then, in the same week, both *Esquire* magazine, a men's publication, and *People* magazine, one of the highest circulation magazines in the country, published editorials urging their readers to take part in Take Our Daughters to Work Day. I knew the massive number of people these magazines reached and what it meant to have their mainstream endorsement of our project. People in positions of power and influence agreed with the need for Take Our Daughters to Work Day. Our vision was resonating far and wide.

Whatever it is you want in your life, start talking about it. Tell people. Share. Slowly but surely, you will begin to find your way. Inevitably, other people will hear something in your idea that resonates with their lives and they will want to be part of your efforts. That is exactly what happened with Take Our Daughters to Work Day. One of the first letters we received after we started publicizing the day came from a nine-year-old girl from Long Island. She wrote that she had been very happy to read about the program in *Parade* magazine, because she had been thinking about the very same kind of day and was so glad someone was going to do it with her.

Imagine if that little girl had had Google. These days, most research and publicity happens on the Internet. Before Internet search engines and computers, I used newspapers and magazines as my research and networking tools. Today, it's all about Google. Nowadays, you can follow political candidates' every triumph and mistake on YouTube. You can find other expectant mothers at three o'clock in the morning on a social networking site. You can organize entire movements simply by starting a blog. It is easier today than ever to connect and communicate and collaborate about anything that interests or excites you. But the prerequisite is knowing what you want, whom you want to find, what words to type into that search engine. You have to search in yourself before searching on Google.

Find Like-Minded People

Facebook and Google Are a Girl's Best Friend

We can all achieve our goals much more quickly and powerfully when we share our goals, resources, and ideas. For whatever you want to achieve, you can count on the fact that other people are working toward the same goal. You can easily find these people through Google searches and social networking sites such as Facebook, MySpace, and LinkedIn.

The Ripple Effect

Did I go into Take Our Daughters to Work Day planning to make history? No. Does anyone, except maybe presidential candidates and Olympic athletes? It is rare to witness history, let alone make it yourself. I don't think Anita Hill came forward with her charges against then–Supreme Court nominee Clarence Thomas knowing that her testimony would make history. Billie Jean King challenged Bobby Riggs to a tennis match mostly to make a point. But these actions did change history, because women pursued issues that mattered to them and tapped into issues that had meaning for large numbers of us. I did not make history with Take Our Daughters to Work Day; we all did. You did. As you will see throughout this book, when one woman makes her own success, the ripple effects are enormous.

The women entrepreneurs participating in the Make Mine a Million $ Business program are encouraged to have big visions for their companies and themselves—and to share their visions with the program's entire community. You may think it's enough to just worry about oneself and one's family—and it is—but the Make Mine a Million $ Business women consistently report that the real breakthroughs in their businesses and personal lives didn't happen until they joined the Make Mine a Million $ Business movement and became part of something bigger than themselves.

Garnett Newcombe was working seven days a week, twelve hours a day, stalled at the same $400,000 in revenue for over three years before she won a place in the Make Mine a Million $ Business community as an award recipient. Her company, Human Potential Consultants (HPC), is a job training and placement agency for veterans returning from Iraq and Afghanistan, for people who have been downsized, and for participants in government disability, welfare, and parole programs.

Garnett knew her business had serious potential but she couldn't see how to grow it. With the program's business coaching and her conversations with members of the community she quickly figured out how to delegate more of her day-to-day work so she could get out and sell her services. In eighteen months Garnett went from $400,000 to $5.7 million in revenue and has contract commitments over the next five years that are worth almost $20 million. By growing her business, she actually improved her own quality of life, working fewer hours to make more money. And she has directly helped and inspired countless other women, including her eighty-eight new employees. According to Count Me In's 2008 research with American Express OPEN, 46 percent of women business owners want to grow their business to help themselves and their families; 48 percent want to grow their businesses to help their community and the world.

As you begin to see your success as part of the larger world, you are also building a support network. Seeing yourself as part of a larger movement also provides extra insurance that resistance won't hold you back. There are moments in every campaign I work on when I feel doubt and even panic. But instead of succumbing to the fears, I reach out for help and start talking to or e-mailing people who are working toward goals that are similar to mine. Every time I do this I am overwhelmed by the passion, excitement, ideas, and resources that women and men share with me.

See Your Life as Part of a Bigger Picture

You are rarely the only one in the world who wants the life you want or has the dreams you have. Access the wider world of people with your interests and goals and use this network for support, encouragement, and an occasional kick in the pants.

Who can you talk to for support? Here are just a few ideas:

- Trusted friends and relatives
- Your significant other, if he or she supports you in this endeavor
- Members of a networking group, professional organization, religious group, or club that you belong to or decide to join, e.g., the National Association of Women Business Owners (www.nawbo.org), your local Chamber of Commerce, or a Curves fitness center (www.curves.com)
- A therapist, life coach, or career coach (check out the Coach Connection at www.findyour coach.com)

- Bloggers, social networking connections, and
members of online discussion boards, such as
iVillage.com, HuffingtonPost.com, or one of the
ever-growing list of "mommy bloggers." Better
yet, launch your own blog (www.blogger.com)
where you record your random musings and big
goals.

Success

On the morning of April 24, 1993, I opened my eyes and
realized that I had nowhere to go. Usually when I organized a big event day, I was up early and at a central location, managing crowds, cops, TV crews, faxes, and
newspaper coverage. But not that day. Though I'd been
working a year and a half for this moment, you'd never
have known it. I was wearing an old T-shirt, lying in bed in
my apartment. Although I had done everything I knew to
make this day a success, without a central rallying point, a
main stage to speak from, or a specific street corner to
meet the public and press, I wasn't sure what to do with
myself.

Still in bed, I picked up the remote and switched on the
television. A little girl in a plaid dress was standing in front
of a map, reporting on a low-pressure system that was
moving from west to east. Her father, the weatherman,
was standing beside her, beaming. She brandished the
pointer as he reported daily highs and lows, and how many

inches of rain we'd had this year. I was mesmerized by the sight of her, filling the screen. "We can expect rain to start somewhere between five and six tomorrow," the girl finished. "For channel five news, this is Laura Fox."

She smiled at her father, who walked back into the frame and said, "This is Take Our Daughters to Work Day." And then a detergent commercial flickered onto the screen and I just cried with joy. Nothing before had ever given me the thrill of this scene on local television: one girl stepping into a place of public power and influence.

The phone rang, and it was a friend standing at Grand Central Terminal, overlooking the concourse. "This place is packed with girls. You can't believe it!" After she hung up, I phoned our project manager, Kristen, and told her, "Turn on the TV!" We began flipping through the channels in tandem. "Oh, my God!" I heard Kristen say.

Daughters were everywhere. They were being interviewed by the newly hired Katie Couric on *The Today Show* with Marie Wilson, president of the Ms. Foundation. They were inspecting dams at the Tennessee Valley Authority. They stood in firehouses in Colorado and in hospital operating rooms in New York. They sat on courtroom benches and at insurance company board meetings. They watched telephones being installed and they rode commuter trains with conductors. They were going behind the scenes at the Metropolitan Opera and lunching at the State Department. They were publishing their own newspaper at the *New York Times,* called the *Girls Times.*

All day, everywhere I went, I encountered swarms of girls, as if an invisible class of society had emerged from its hive of anonymity. Later that night, I hosted a party at my home office to celebrate. We were glued to the television—every network was featuring Take Our Daughters to Work Day on the evening news. Just that morning, I had started out in that same room, alone. That night I sat in a circle of celebration, watching images of girls from all over the country flash across the screen.

The next morning I woke up to that call from Wyatt Andrews on the Washington to New York shuttle.

Over a million people had taken their daughters into workplaces. Within the space of a day, we had successfully made a shift in the culture. Girls made the news that night and were featured on the front of every major newspaper the next morning—not because they were cute, kittenish consumers, not because they had low self-esteem or anorexia or addiction problems, but because they were curious, visible, and full of potential.

We had shown the world that girls—our daughters— are the future workforce, political force, employers, leaders, and constituents. And best of all, the world had listened. A door had swung open that had long separated the private and public worlds, and little girls—so long unexposed and invisible—had walked through.

Because of that first day and each Take Our Daughters to Work Day since, girls can see what is possible outside of their homes, schools, and romantic fantasies. And prospective employers, parents, and teachers have begun to view girls as future entrepreneurs, valued employees, and leaders. Girls have been inspired to imagine a wider landscape, a new kind of future for themselves.

To me, that is what it looks like to change the world—my world, your world, and the world of all of our daughters.

Take Our Daughters to Work Day

Have you taken part in Take Our Daughters to Work Day—the first one, the fifth one, or any one? I always love to hear people's stories about their experiences and how the day affected them. E-mail me your Take Our Daughters to Work Day story at nm@countmein.org.

In the chapters that follow, we'll explore the lessons of Take Our Daughters to Work Day in more detail and apply these lessons to the success that you want to achieve in your life—whether you want to make big changes, small changes, or medium-sized changes. I hope you are now confident in the knowledge that virtually anything is possible and you can define success any way you'd like. In the next chapter, I'll let you in on a fabulous secret: when you begin to make changes in your life, the world changes around you.

THE SYSTEM IS MORE MALLEABLE
THAN YOU THINK

When you decide to step out of line at home, at work, in your community, or in the world, you are not just changing your own life. You are changing a larger system. For instance, when you date online, you are changing the system of believing that Prince Charming will come knocking on your door. When you speak up about the horror of landmines, you are changing the system that says that governments are more powerful than individuals. When you participate in Take Our Daughters to Work Day, you are changing the system that says girls should be seen and not heard.

One of the biggest lessons I've learned from creating big social change campaigns is that the system is far more malleable than we think. Families morph. Structures shift. Bureaucracies jiggle and rattle and roll. Fashions change. Barriers fall. This chapter is full of examples of how rules and laws transform because people want them to. Whatever systemic barriers you feel you're facing, you'll see that they are malleable, too.

Systems Change Because People Change Them

Every time you step out of line and take action on behalf of your personal goals, you are changing the system. When you live your life according to your vision, other women see that it is possible, and they know they can do it, too.

The women of the Make Mine a Million $ Business community are changing the system every day. They are reaching across barriers and doing business according to their own rules. Mary Ardapple owns Apple's Bakery (www.applesbakery.com) in Peoria, Illinois. She is an active member of her Chamber of Commerce, a mother, and a Make Mine a Million $ Business award winner. A description of Mary's business, along with her photograph, appears on the MakeMineaMillion.org Web site. Nandini Mukherjee, owner of the Indian Bread Company (www.indianbreadco.com) in New York City, read Mary's story as she was filling out her application for the Make Mine a Million $ Business program. Nandini reached out to Mary, because she was also in the food business, for advice and mentoring. Mary happily shared some tips and, when she arrived in New York to attend the Make Mine a Million $

Business event where Nandini was competing, she stopped by Nandini's restaurant to say hello and taste her food.

Nandini applied Mary's advice to describe her mouth-watering, innovative, handheld Indian sandwiches to the judges and the live voting audience, and she won. Mary had shared her secret to success in the competition with Nandini; Nandini graciously took the advice and now both women are successful. Many people approach business as a world of fear, scarcity, secrets, and greed. Mary and Nandini made their own rules of business—a system in which everybody can win.

When I Think About Changing the System, I Think About Changing Pants

In the early 1960s, an attractive woman approached the entrance to the famous Four Seasons Restaurant in New York City. She wore a fashionable tunic and pants along with big black Jackie O–style sunglasses. The maître d' stopped her. "I'm sorry, madam," he said, "but we do not allow women in pants into our establishment."

"I see," the woman said. She thought for a moment, then excused herself to the ladies' room, where she pulled off her pants and came back to the maître d' stand—wearing only her tunic, which served as a micro-mini dress.

The maître d' promptly escorted her to a table.

I heard this story from my best friend's mother. She absolutely loves talking about that woman at the Four Seasons. And it's the story that always comes to my mind when women question what is possible in our world.

Pants are a great example of the system being far more malleable than we think.

When I was a little girl in the 1960s, I went to Catholic school every day for eleven years wearing some version of a plaid skirt and knee socks, and I wore dresses and little white gloves to church on Sunday. Even on the coldest days, we wore dresses with pants underneath. But over the years, women started wearing pants to church. The church never decreed that trousers were acceptable. There was no edict from the pope. Eventually, people just gave up on what had always been done and women started wearing pants if they felt like it.

When I visited my older sister, Claire, at Barnard College in 1968, I saw the system change right in front of me. Her dorm, across the street from the famous Columbia University campus, went from all girls and no boys allowed upstairs when she started, to men being there all the time. Grades for courses disappeared. So did bras. Claire and I went to Woodstock together. In just a few years, the world went from white gloves to Woodstock. From knee socks to no bra.

I wore dresses and skirts for years—I have good legs and wanted to show off my best feature. But I can probably count on one hand the times I have worn a skirt in the past fifteen years. I got steadily into pants when I started my own business in 1988. I grew more comfortable and confident wearing pants and covering my legs. And who wanted to wear pantyhose, anyway? One of the few times

I've worn a skirt in the past fifteen years was the day I got married.

Changing the System of Marriage

I'm honestly not sure if it's a more shocking fact that I wore a skirt or that I got married. From 1968 onward, I never thought much about getting married. I was living in a world with no grades, no sex-segregated dorms, no bras, and no weddings. Marriage wasn't a huge tradition in my family either. The only wedding I remember seeing in family photo albums was my Aunt Connie's second marriage, a very glamorous New York affair. I was too young to attend, but Claire was there with my parents. My mother and father didn't have a big wedding; there are no photos, no dress, no nothing.

In my twenties, with birth control and jobs opening up for women everywhere, why get married? I thought it was too patriarchal. I was too independent, had too many other things to do with my life. How could I be a wife? I decided sometime in college that the whole system of marriage was simply not in my future.

Clearly, I didn't see marriage as a malleable system. That's not too surprising. I'm not sure there is any system in our society that is more fundamental and more deeply ingrained than the notion that a girl grows up, meets a man, gets married, and has children. It's a strong belief system because a lot of people are very happy following that path—and, of course, we wouldn't carry on a society without people procreating! But it is a system nonetheless, and a system with deeply—deeply—ingrained rituals, beliefs, and support structures. I am an example: rather than thinking I could change marriage to suit my vision of it, I instead believed that marriage was not for me.

Starting and owning my own business is what convinced me that I wanted to be in a committed relationship. I liked running my own business so much more than working for someone else in a frustrating bureaucracy. Working at home and building my business, I started to carve out a life besides work—I was spending time with my family, going to the gym regularly, entertaining friends. I was in therapy. I was thinking about what I wanted to do and how I could help my clients, and I felt in control of my time and money. Now that I had all of this, I wanted to share it with someone.

Gary and I met in May 1992, a full year before the first Take Our Daughters to Work Day. The relationship developed along with that big event, which turned out to be a tremendous public success and also a personal success. It changed me. I now knew that I could create and execute a campaign that changed the culture. My self-confidence improved. We set a goal and engaged people across the country to help make it happen. And the media, people like the CBS reporter Wyatt Andrews and the editors of major newspapers, plus corporate leaders and politicians, deemed it a success, too. Gary was certainly impressed with the success of it, but he never let me get a swelled head. He liked me and was happy to be with me, success or not.

As you learned in the Introduction, Gary and I met on a blind date set up by my accountant. Gary was sitting at the restaurant's bar waiting for me when I walked in. I was late for our date and definitely a little nervous. But when I walked in the door, a few people I knew came up and said hello to me before I could even check in. It's always nice to run into people, but I was slightly mortified. "What is this guy going to think of me?" I thought. "Is he going to be intimidated? Irritated?"

I couldn't have been more wrong. Gary loved it. I learned later that he was sitting at the bar watching this scene, and thinking, "Wow. Who is that woman? Why does everybody know her?" He told me there is nothing more attractive than a woman with confidence.

There Is Nothing More Attractive than a Woman with Confidence

I married the man who said this to me. And I would advise you to look for a partner with the same opinion.

It wasn't until I met Gary that I believed marriage could exist on my terms—that it could fit my life, my personality, and my goals. I didn't have to change to get married; marriage could change. And yet, even on my wedding day, I worried that I couldn't be a wife and that I was giving up my independence.

Right before the ceremony, I locked myself in the bathroom, staring at my image in the mirror. There I was in a cream-colored skirt suit that I'd bought at a store called—believe it or not—the Forgotten Woman. I loved the suit, particularly the jacket, which was gorgeous and elegant, with flowers appliquéd on the bodice and shoulders. I stood, barely recognizing myself, as the New Yorker who always wears black, thinking I looked like an off-white refrigerator. What was I doing in a skirt? What was I doing getting married? This wasn't me! My best friend Beth had to talk me out of the bathroom and reassure me that it would be okay.

I went through with the wedding, of course. And once I got out there, we had a wonderful time. My face hurt from smiling. And I can say that marriage has been more than I ever imagined. I am still independent and still outspoken, and now I have a loving, giving companion to share life with.

Our marriage is what my husband and I want it to be, which sometimes conforms to traditional wife and husband roles, and often doesn't. We each kept the names we had when we met. We maintain separate bank accounts. Gary does most of the grocery shopping and cooking. We do not have children together, and I am grateful and fortunate to be the stepmother to his grown children, Nick and Laura.

Logistical issues aside, I think we interact in our

unique way as well. It's hard to describe one's own relationship, so I'll use the description sent to me by my friend Isisara Bey, whom you'll read more about later. After an evening with Gary and me, she wrote: "They enjoy each other, support each other, are graceful and gracious to each other, and are yielding to each other while standing firm and strong in their own essences. I see gratitude between them for each other and for what they have." Our marriage is a union of two people who want to be ourselves and want to be a couple. It's not what I thought marriage would be. It's what I hoped marriage could be.

Love

I'm far from the only one who has grappled with the changing mores of love and marriage. I was reminded of this on the first Take Our Daughters to Work Day when I attended an event at New York's City Hall to be with a class of seventh-grade girls from a junior high school down the street. The girls were meeting all the highest ranking women in Mayor David Dinkins's administration during a ceremony in the city council chamber.

Bella Abzug, one of my heroes, was on hand in her role as director of the New York City Commission on the Status of Women (now the NYC Commission on Women's Issues, www.nyc.gov/html/cwi). She spoke to the girls about how much the world had changed for women since her birth in the 1920s and how much more needed to be done. She talked about her early days as a lawyer, when she was one of only two women in her law school class, about going to court for the first time when she was eight months pregnant, and running for Congress at the age of fifty. It was classic Bella—blunt and heartfelt.

As she was finishing, a skinny girl with thick glasses sitting in the front row raised her hand to ask a question. Bella pointed to her, and she stood.

"Did your husband laugh at you when you came home and told him you wanted to run for Congress?" she asked.

Bella took off her own glasses and smiled, then leaned into the podium so she was eye-to-eye with the girl. "I think we need to spend some time talking about how to pick out the right kind of fella," she said.

The adults burst out laughing, but the girls sat at rapt attention waiting for Bella's formula.

Bella told them it was important to find someone who appreciated them for who they were, who valued what was under the surface. She told them that looks are important in seventh grade, but they become less so as you grow older. And she advised them to look for the kind of person who could be a friend and partner for life. Then she spoke about her husband, Martin, who had been all those things to her, who had joined with her in raising their daughters while they practiced law and who had recently died. There was a long moment of stillness, and then the audience began to applaud.

Those seventh-grade girls were very astute: we don't get a lot of helpful information about picking the right life partner. We're told the right person will "come along when you least expect it!" We hear about love at first sight on airplanes or in hotel lounges. Songs tell us, "One day he'll come along . . . the man I love." For centuries, women have waited and waited and waited for these things to happen—for the system to deliver on its promise. And for some women, the right partner does just come along. But for many, many, many more women, it takes some work.

I got a little lucky. I met my husband on a fix-up. That's more modern than the historical system of arranged marriages, but it's still pretty traditional. I was very clear, though, that I wanted a man who loved me because of, not despite, my independence.

This is a far cry from how I thought about men—well, boys—when I was in sixth grade and still wearing skirts every day. I'd daydream about the cute boys in my class. I regularly constructed an entire life, complete with handsome husband, kids, house, and wardrobe in a matter of seconds. I'll bet you did this too.

I remember one boy in particular, George, a shy, smart boy with slicked-back hair, who sat next to me in the middle of our sixth-grade year. Within minutes, I'd turned him into my personal romantic hero, imbuing him with bravery, sensitivity, creativity, pouring into him all my longings. I sketched a plunging neckline dress that I'd wear with him on some undefined elementary school evening. I kissed my own forearm in a rehearsal of how I would one day kiss him on the lips.

I visualized my new Marilyn Monroe figure and the duplex we'd live in with our three children. I created this intricate world in just a few seconds of reverie in math class, in spite of the fact that George rarely looked my way or uttered a word.

Obviously, I've changed a lot since sixth grade, but too many women still use this approach to meet a partner and construct a life: dreaming and fantasizing. Sure, that has its place, but it's not an effective strategy for finding a love partner. It used to be that we didn't have much choice, unless we wanted to hang out in a singles bar every night. Today, the system for meeting people has changed completely—all thanks to online dating. We've gone from fix-ups to fixing ourselves up. Instead of waiting and hoping for a mate to come along, or relying on anyone from your Aunt Annie or your accountant to offer a match, you can step out of line and go online to search for the precise kind of partner you want.

THE NEW SYSTEM OF SEARCHING FOR LOVE

Want to know how malleable the system of dating has become? Check out the variety of dating Web sites that exist. Looking for a Catholic mate? Try CatholicSingles.com. A Jewish mate? JDate.com. A lesbian partner? Grrl2grrl.com. An eco-friendly mate? Green-Passions.com. A fellow single parent? Single ParentLove.com. A Latino life partner? Amigos.com. Only interested in dating a fellow golfer? There's GolfMates.com. If there was ever a stigma against online dating, the depth of niche dating sites like these is one major sign that the stigma is over. The numbers confirm it. According to Mark J. Penn in his 2007 book, *Microtrends,* "Internet Marrieds" are a major force in society:

- Nearly one in four single Americans—16 million people—use more than one thousand dating Web sites to meet people.
- Seventeen percent of online daters—nearly 3 million Americans—have turned online dates into a long-term relationship or marriage.
- Internet marriage can happen for anyone. Fifty-five percent are under age thirty-five and forty-six percent are over thirty-five, including almost a third who are over forty-five. It works for second-timers, too: thirty-one percent of Internet Marrieds are on their second marriage.

If that doesn't constitute a new system for finding mates and marriage partners, then I don't know what does. And it seems we are pretty good at setting ourselves up: a remarkable ninety-two percent of Internet Marrieds say their marriages are happy.

My opinion is that online matches succeed because you're practically forced into creating your own customized definition of a successful relationship. When you register for a dating site, you are invited to fill out a ton of information about yourself and the kind of person you'd like to meet: Is he a smoker? Does she like animals and if so, which ones? Do you want children? Is it okay if your match has children already? How often do you go to temple? Do you go to church every Sunday or only on Christmas and Easter? What's his or her education level? Political persuasion? Age range that is acceptable to you? What do you like to do in your free time? Favorite foods? Description of the perfect first date? Body shape that best describes your ideal partner? Do you want to date for fun? To get married and have a family? Just for "random play"? It's entirely up to you to define what you want and to go after it.

Dating and mating are no longer about chemistry, magic, and luck, at least not at first. Those things are glorious, but if your vision of success involves a fabulous life partner, then you've got to start taking matters into your own hands and stop waiting for love to find you. Women today are so fortunate to have a system that allows us to seek out our own mates simply by clicking a mouse. All it takes is the confidence to believe you can have what you want. Infinite potential partners are available right at your fingertips, so you can stop waiting and start dating.

EXERCISE: Write Your Own "Life Ad"

Online dating is a great metaphor for how systems can change. Today you can advertise for the person of your dreams. Wouldn't it be great if you could write an online dating profile for other areas of your life too? Remember, online dating ads are incredibly specific, very detailed, and full of you describing what you want in your own words—full of colors and aromas and feelings and quirks.

Go ahead and write an ad for how you'd like your life to look. Here is an example:

SEEKING: NEW JOB

My sales director position is with a respected pharmaceutical company that is listed in the "100 Best Companies for Working Mothers." The company is incredibly supportive of parents and is happy for me to telecommute or work flexible hours when I need to. They have an onsite day-care center that is high-quality and affordable. There are several high-profile women in senior management, and the company has a respected policy of equal pay for equal work. I feel comfortable there as a mom and as a businesswoman. My office is styled with large windows, lots of bookshelves, and a deliciously comfortable Aeron chair. I have plants on my windowsill that thrive in the sunlight and good vibes. I am provided with a BlackBerry and super-light laptop that doesn't hurt my shoulders to carry, and the company helps set me up to work from home when I need to. The corporate environment is the antithesis of The Office; people are smart, friendly, motivated, and eager to help one another. The office has a productive buzz in the air—with people working hard and enjoying their work. I make some new friends and have ambitious employees to mentor. The company provides delicious gourmet coffee and has fresh fruit available in the kitchen. My paychecks are 30 percent higher than what I am making now, with the company matching my monthly 401(k) contributions. My boss is experienced, smart, and likes his or her employees to have a personal life. I am happy and grow in this position, allowing me to rise to the next level in my career.

Now it's your turn. Write your own personal ad for any area of your life or all areas of your life. Be as creative and ambitious as you'd like and remember to include feelings, sights, sounds, and smells. Remember, you can't have what you want until you can define it.

SEEKING:

Legally Sitting Naked in a Park

Let's widen our lens now to historical and political systems. We don't just live in a bubble with the people we love. We each play a role in civil society as well. Stepping out of line means standing up for oneself and issues bigger than oneself. We all lead by example. So much of what women are achieving today, and what we can imagine about the future, was built on the shoulders of the women who came before us.

Some of those shoulders were naked at the Women's Bathing Pond in London's Hampstead Heath. I discovered this magical place when I was twenty-four years old and studying labor relations in the British National Health Service on a Fulbright scholarship. Think of Hampstead Heath as the Central Park of London.

To find the pond for the first time, my friend Linda and I followed a map that led down a long path where we eventually spotted a little sign covered with leaves. Past the sign, we came upon a clearing washed in sunlight and surrounded by high trees. There I saw dozens of naked women of all shapes and ages lounging on the grass and a brave few swimming in the icy cold water. Not wanting to stand out, we quickly took off all our clothes and joined this glorious group in all our nakedness. It was like walking onto a movie set—can you imagine coming across a bunch of naked women sunbathing on a hillside in the middle of Central Park?

Eventually, we struck up a conversation with one of the women, who seemed ancient to me—she was probably in her late eighties or nineties. She was a delightful sight: she wore plastic water shoes, sported nothing but a bath towel pinned as a cape around her shoulders, and held on to a shopping cart as a walker. As we slowly walked and talked, it emerged that she was the daughter of an English suffragette. She explained to me that in her mother's day, there was a male bathing pond on the Heath. Women wanted everything that men had, just as they wanted the right to vote, so the women wanted their own bathing pond. Thanks in part to this woman's mother, they fought for it and got it. (They planted higher trees around its perimeter, to keep away the peeping Toms. Today cell phones and radios are banned to keep out any stressful noise.)

"This woman's pond is one of the many things my mother fought for," the caped old woman told me.

The Women's Bathing Pond exists because women like my acquaintance's mother didn't wait for what they wanted. They were fighting for something very important—the right to vote—and they wanted what men had. Men have a public bathing pond? We want a public bathing pond! The only difference in the ponds is the high trees surrounding the women's place—a nod to the fact that equal doesn't always mean identical.

As women of our great-grandmothers' generation fought for and won the right to vote and the right to swim naked in the center of London, surely we must continue this tradition by expanding our role and influence in every aspect of life. Those women created a place in a public park where women could swim. In Victorian England! That had a deep impact on them, their daughters, their sons, and the future. If they could do it, we can too. And we have it much, much easier. They didn't have the power of blogs and bulletin boards or even long-distance calling!

How would these women, our great-grandmothers feel if they walked out of the past into the middle of our modern lives, dragging their brooms and hoes, wearing long aprons, careworn and elderly by forty, which was the life expectancy for women in 1875?

Having been voteless and voiceless in their own time, they would be amazed that our lives are no longer dominated by pregnancy, that we no longer bear a dozen or more children, that childbirth is not the most common cause of our deaths. They would be astonished by our liberation from the sheer domestic drudgery that took up their own lives—our freedom from sheet boiling, fire tending, rug beating, bread baking. They would be proud to see us driving our own cars, owning our own businesses, presiding at corporate meetings, owning not only rooms of our own, but whole apartments and houses. It would be impossible to tear them away from Google.

And yet, they might also be shocked at how unaware many women are of the distance we have traveled in only a few generations, and how blasé we have become about rights and freedoms that earlier generations of women fought hard for. They would be puzzled at how few of us vote (in the 2004 presidential election, 8 million women registered but did not vote), when it took seventy long years of struggle to obtain the right to pull the lever at the polls. They would be shaken by how many women are forfeiting their excellent educations, turning their backs on the public arena in order to retreat into domestic life because the challenges of juggling child rearing and career seem too insurmountable. They would be dismayed by how much time and money we spend not on securing our retirement futures, but on our looks—chasing youth and beauty with loads of products and procedures.

Most of all, they might be particularly surprised and dismayed by the most enduring legacy from our powerless past: our own self-limiting behaviors. They would find disturbing how many women still hedge their bets, back away from opportunity and success at the last moment and fail to advance the final mile—how many women fail to step out of line. They would urge us to think bigger, achieve our every desire, be strong, successful, powerful women. They would encourage us not to back off while someone else takes the prize. They would tell us to stop waiting and start living the exact lives we want. They would encourage us not to let systems, bureaucracies, or traditions stand in our way.

When you really stop and think about how much has changed since our great-grandmothers' times, you realize that anything really is possible. The status quo is malleable in every aspect of life. And yet, the pace of progress can be frustratingly slow. In her *New York Times* column endorsing Take Our Daughters to Work Day, Anna Quindlen eloquently captured how much has changed for women, and yet how much still hasn't. Quindlen presented her argument on March 28, 1993, around a woman who is still a touchstone for these issues today—Hillary Clinton:

> Maybe some of our daughters took notice of how Hillary Clinton was seen as abrasive, power-hungry, and unfeminine when to some of us she seemed merely smart, outspoken, and hardworking. Maybe they saw the masquerade and recognized intuitively the age-old message about how much more attractive women are when they are domestic, soft, contented, the message aimed over the years at Susan

B. Anthony, Margaret Sanger, Eleanor Roosevelt
and many, many others . . .

It's better than it used to be. Just as most of us
can't tell our kids stories about walking five miles
through the snow to school, so many of us can't lay
claim to the problems of an earlier generation, in
which women who graduated from law school were
sometimes offered a secretary's job at a law firm.
But still our young girls, like our First Woman, often
get contradictory and hostile messages about their
lives, their futures, and their selves.

I was fascinated to discover during the writing of this
book, fifteen years later, on June 14, 2008, that Quindlen
wrote a column with a similar message for *Newsweek* in
the wake of Hillary Clinton's loss to Barack Obama: "Sometimes being an older woman at this moment in time can
be a bit like one of those dreams in which you're running
hard and yet not moving. On the one hand, we've come so
far. On the other, there's always that fear of being dragged
back to the bad old ways, in which the crust on our
casseroles and the size of our breasts were how we were
measured."

When I start to feel outraged by the slow pace of
progress, I take a moment to remember how far women
have come, even in the microcosm of my family. Just look
at how much has changed between my great-grandmother's
time and my own:

My Maternal Great-Grandmother Mary Degan Ryan	Me
Born 1859 at home in Trenton, NJ	Born 1953 in St. Francis Hospital in Trenton, NJ
Gave birth to five children and adopted a neighborhood boy whose parents died in the influenza epidemic	Stepmother of two
Did not attend high school or college	Went to college a year early and was a Fulbright Scholar in England
Never cast a vote	Have voted since age eighteen and worked in national politics
Never worked outside the home, but made all her children's clothes, meals, and bread daily	Have worked outside the home since age sixteen
Made the most beautiful crazy quilt I've ever seen. It hung in my house as a child.	Can't sew a hem, but have a bag of material saved for that some- day when I'll have time to make a crazy quilt
Never traveled far from Trenton, NJ	Have traveled to thirty-eight states in the U.S. and all continents ex- cept Antarctica. Lived in London at age nineteen.
Was an incredible baker	Love to bake cakes

EXERCISE: Change through the Generations

Now it's your turn. Think about your knowledge of what life was like for your own grandmothers or great-grandmothers—both how much has changed and the threads that carry through. If you don't know your family history and have no relatives to ask, check out the Web site Ancestry.com, which can help you build a family tree.

My Great-Grandmother	Me

Keeping a Sense of Humor with the Dinosaurs

So much changes and can change, and yet, so much stays the same. Many systems that affect women's lives have barely changed at all since our great-grandmothers' times. For instance, women are still rare in traditionally male-dominated industries such as construction, engineering, and trucking. I'll never forget a story in a speech I heard by Governor Janet Napolitano of Arizona. She told about a friend of hers, a woman who was appointed by then Texas governor Ann Richards to be head of the state's trucking commission. She didn't know much about the industry and spent several nights cramming for her first meeting with the Texas truckers. On the appointed day, she delivered her speech and opened the floor to questions from the almost all male audience of truckers.

"I have a question," one man said as he walked up to the microphone. "What's your bra size?"

I'm sure many people expected for the woman to cry or blush or walk off the stage in a huff. Instead, she ignored him. But when reporters asked her later what she thought of the question she said: "I'm just glad he asked me a question I knew the answer to!"

Humor is a powerful tool when it comes to changing the system. If you're thinking, "I wish I could come up with lines like that!" you are not alone. And my response is, you can learn things to say instead of walking away from confrontation. Study women you admire! Watch old movies of Joan Crawford and Bette Davis and Katharine Hepburn. It's okay to have a few "comebacks" in your pocket in case you ever need them.

Sometimes comments like this happen in the glare of the public eye. During the primary season leading up to the 2008 presidential election, a news story spread about an incident that took place at a Hillary Clinton rally in New Hampshire. While Clinton, a United States senator, was giving a speech, two men yelled out from the crowd, "Iron my shirt!"

Now, that is the kind of thing that could drive me—and

most women—crazy. But when I saw this story on the news, instead of wanting to deck those guys, I started to think about how backward the idea of ironing even was. Hadn't they heard of permanent press? How about drip dry? Not to mention the fact that dry cleaning is really inexpensive these days, and it's even green.

You can waste a lot of time being furious at people like these guys. But if you really want to change the system, rather than being angry at misogynists, focus your attention on alternatives. In this case, I started to think about all the ways that women have found to avoid ironing. Over the years we have made our lack of desire and time to iron so clear that it has changed how fabrics are manufactured (think Lycra and anything created by Eileen Fisher) and companies have developed whole clothing lines that are no-iron. The simple fact is that the guys who heckled Clinton at that rally are dinosaurs. The system has already changed and left them behind. No wonder they are yelling.

Changing Law Firm Culture

It's worth thinking some more about those men in Senator Clinton's audience. Who has more power to change the world—a U.S. senator from New York or two guys heckling? Those guys don't have much power. They just have loud voices. The issue of power—and who has it—makes me think of Carol, a brilliant young lawyer who asked me out to lunch for some advice about her career.

Elegant and articulate, Carol was the only senior female associate left at her global white-shoe law firm; all the rest of her contemporaries had quit or left to have babies. Two years away from becoming a partner, she was a brilliant litigator and had outperformed her boss in a mock trial that would ultimately be worth billions of dollars to a client. When her boss, the head of litigation, made his argument, 30 percent of the jury believed it. When Carol addressed the jury, 70 percent believed her.

Yet she was thinking of leaving the law.

"But why?" I asked her.

"The atmosphere—it's so male dominated and corporate. Everything's driven by the billable hour."

What she really wanted, she told me, was to develop an international micro-lending organization in her native country. She said that this would answer her need for a higher purpose.

Because I ran a micro-lending organization, she thought I would be full of encouragement and information. To her surprise, I didn't encourage her to change careers, but instead to persevere in the one for which she was so clearly gifted.

"Why don't you stay on at the law firm on your own terms? Tell the partners exactly what you want. Write a proposal for a flextime plan, or a sabbatical program, or a pro bono project that works with international micro businesses. Do it just like you would write a brief for a big case. Make your argument, persuade them. And once you become a partner you can set up hundreds of micro-lending organizations from your powerful position."

Carol was shocked. It hadn't occurred to her to ask for what she really wanted. She thought if she wanted something different she would have to go. She couldn't see that she was part of the deal-closing, money-making system and had power to influence it and change it.

It is easier to make change from a position of power, which is part of the reason I encouraged Carol to remain at her law firm. In law firms, the power center is clear: The partners have the power. In other organizations or situations, the power locus might not be as obvious. In that case, you need to find the power if you want to make change. Find the power, and then ask yourself how far removed you are from that center. How many steps removed are you from the power center at your office? In your community? What do you think it would take to get closer to that power, if that's something that interests you? These are questions to ask yourself if you are interested in changing a situation, job, law, or anything else.

If you have trouble defining where power is located, do some research. If Carol conducted a quick Internet search, she would find that other women lawyers feel the same way that she does. The San Francisco–based law firm Heller Ehrman, for example, has created the Opt-In Project (www.hellerehrman.com/optin), which studies how law firms do business and how that affects women. The project even discussed the abolition of the billable hour— a long-standing, deeply ingrained practice. "We can't afford to keep losing all these people," Patricia Gillette, founder of the project, commented in Lisa Belkin's May 17, 2007 *New York Times* article, "After Baby, Boss Comes

Calling." "The way we currently reward spending more and more hours at work makes no sense in a world where people demand balance." The firm now holds "Beyond the Billable Hour" roundtable discussions with general counsels and law firm managing partners to discuss ways in which law firms can better serve clients through alternative billing arrangements that may facilitate work-life balance.

The American Bar Association estimates that 90 percent of law firms charge by the billable hour, but the "anti-billable hour" crusade seems to be spreading. In October 2007, a small law firm in Boston decided to ban the billable hour. Shepherd Law Group (www.shepherdlawgroup.com), an employment law firm, now charges clients either a flat annual fee or a fixed price for a specific task.

It's Easier to Make Change from a Position of Power

Don't stand on the outside with your nose pressed to the glass, excluded. Determine where the power is, and make some assessment as to whether—and how—you can get into the action. What power do you already have, and what could you use it to achieve?

Be All You Can Be

I know a lot about power because I grew up with it— power and politics were my family business. It's always been clear to me that I needed to figure out who had the power, whether it was on the playground or in a presidential campaign. I never ran for office but I've used everything I know about politics to achieve so much I've done.

Power is not a comfortable topic for many women. Thanks to relatives, teachers, friends, and the media, we all grow up with some notion of what power and success means for boys and what it means for girls. For boys, power and success are usually about achieving in sports or growing tall, strong, and powerful. For girls, it's often still about being pretty and nice, and having boys like us. In the 2007 obituary of Deborah Kerr, the actress is quoted as saying, "I don't think anyone knew I could act until I put on a bathing suit." In a 2007 *New York Times* article about the pressures on teenage girls, one high school girl named Kat said, " 'It's out of style to admit it, but it is more important to be hot than smart.

" 'Effortlessly hot,' Kat added."

Who can live up to the pressure to be "effortlessly hot"!

One of the most wonderful lessons of Take Our Daughters to Work Day was how girls don't see any problem with being beautifully feminine and having a high-impact career. In the months leading up to the first year of Take Our Daughters to Work Day, we received free advertisements in *Barbie* magazine. The ads invited the girls to participate in the day and send back a form to get the brochure for their teacher, parents, and their parent's employer. On the form we asked for their name and address and there was a space for girls to tell us what they wanted to be when they grew up. We got hundreds of handwritten forms back from girls between the ages of six and eight telling us what they wanted to be and it was regularly two wildly different jobs. Girls wrote in that they wanted to be "a scientist and a fashion model," "a veterinarian and a movie actress," "a doctor and a princess" or "a fireman and a ballerina."

It was too prevalent a trend to be anything but authentic. Girls were clear about wanting to be in a serious/helping profession combined with a glamorous job. What a powerful combination of ways to think about yourself as a brilliant, beautiful, caring, hardworking citizen.

As we grow older, we are surrounded by messages and images telling us that, for men, success is a lucrative job and prominent position in society. For women, it's getting married and having children and a well-kept home—often while staying slim and attractive and, these days, having a lucrative career as well. Just think of how many people pointed to former First Lady Laura Bush as the picture of "perfect" womanhood. In this day and age, how many women have lives like Laura Bush? It is certainly one choice to be a full-time wife who claims not to have any involvement in her husband's work, but it is nowhere near the standard of life for women today.

Traditional notions of success for women are deeply ingrained, but the reality is that the definition of success is more fluid. Even the dictionary is pretty vague and open-ended about it, providing the definition: "wealth, position, honors, or the like." But, in the absence of your providing your own "like," you're at risk of defaulting into thinking that success has a very narrow and stagnant definition.

I heard Ann Curry, the *Today Show* news anchor, give a speech at *More* magazine's Reinvention Conference where she told the audience that, although she loved her children deeply, she doesn't say that their births were the most satisfying moments of her life. She said that the moments she has spent helping others in the world, particularly the stories she broadcast about the suffering in Kosovo, have been more satisfying and important to her, because she helped millions of people. Clearly, she knows that the default answer to the "most satisfying moments" question is either your wedding day or the birth of your children. Those are incredibly important and significant experiences, but there are many, many others as well. Why do we even feel pressure to prioritize moments in this way? Your satisfaction is your business.

Little girls get this. Left to their own perceptions, many girls today can see the world differently. My four-year-old niece Maggie says it's boring to watch old-fashioned cartoons where the girl mouse is always tied to the railroad tracks. "Why is the girl screaming for help?" she asked her father, my brother Jimmy, while watching an episode of Mighty Mouse. "Why isn't she like Dora [the Explorer], who can take care of herself?"

Maggie is the system now.

Most women would say we want girls like Maggie to live whatever kind of lives they want, to have all the success in the world. And yet, so many women don't allow themselves to have the same thing. It's true that we want what's best for our daughters, but it's also true that our daughters learn by watching us. If we don't look deep inside ourselves to decide what we want in this world and how we're going to get it, our daughters won't believe their own success is possible.

Be More like Dora

Take a confidence lesson from a little girl. Get rid of any lingering images of what women, mothers, daughters, sisters, wives, girlfriends, or superheroes should be, and live more like Dora the Explorer—explore and act with your own courage and bravery.

Just look again at how far we've come: We've gone from a world in my mother's time where most young women didn't go to college to a world today where more than half of college students are female. We've gone from checking out potential mates in our congregations to meeting in bars, to Googling people before first dates. We've gone from growing our own food, to shopping in local markets, to Super Stop-n-Shops, to replenishing our cupboards with one click on Peapod.com or FreshDirect.com. We've gone from lack of birth control, to the pill, to freezing our eggs and "shopping" for male DNA in sperm banks. We've gone from no women tennis players, to Billie Jean King beating Bobby Riggs, to Venus Williams being the first woman to earn the same Wimbledon prize money as a man. Sometimes it takes three minutes and sometimes it takes thirty years, but the system is always more malleable than we think.

3

IMAGINATION IS ESSENTIAL

When I think about imagination, I think about Eddie Murphy. He is a master of imagination. *Trading Places, Coming to America,* and *Dr. Dolittle* are some of my favorite movies. In *Trading Places,* Murphy's character is a homeless man who can imagine himself as a successful commodities broker. In *Coming to America,* Murphy imagines an entire kingdom in Africa—Zamunda—where he is the prince, named Akeem. He awakes to an orchestra of live musicians and beautiful women saying "Good morning, your highness." Wherever he walks, rose petals are scattered in his path. Topless women bathe him in a reflecting pond, a servant brushes his teeth, and another servant acts as his "royal wiper" in the bathroom. As all of this is taking place, elephants pass by the windows outside the palace.

The movie begins on Prince Akeem's twenty-first birthday, the day on which he is to be married to a woman selected by his father, the king, played by James Earl Jones.

The potential bride—impeccably gorgeous with enormous hair and a gold dress with a mile-long train—is presented. She has been trained since birth to please Akeem, but he decides he wants to select his own wife. "Times must, and always do, change," Akeem tells his father.

And so he ventures off to—where else?—Queens, New York, to find his future queen.

In Queens, Murphy imagines himself as an African prince in New York for the first time—marveling at the rude cabdrivers, rat-infested apartments, and neurotic women. As an actor, he takes on several other parts in the film: a talkative barber, a James Brown–style soul singer in a powder blue tuxedo, and even an old Jewish man kvetching at the barbershop.

By the end of the film, Prince Akeem has found his gorgeous, smart, charity-minded American woman. Akeem's mother convinces his father to change the law stating that their son must marry a local girl, and Akeem marries his true love back home in Zamunda. She wears an enormous bubble-gum pink gown and surely the couple lives happily ever after with the elephants and the orchestral alarm clock.

Eddie Murphy created movies where he put himself in positions of power, responsibility, respect, and joy. In *Coming to America,* Murphy also imagined a world where a woman can be powerful, smart, compassionate, and beautiful—he rejects a beautiful woman who does not have a mind of her own. In the 2002 film *The Adventures of Pluto Nash,* Murphy plays a nightclub owner on the moon in the year 2087. When he checks out some newly issued $10,000 dollar bills, they feature the face of Hillary Clinton. He is the first to imagine "Hillary" taking the place of "Benjamins," $100 bills featuring the face of Benjamin Franklin. In his imagination of powerful black men, he also imagines powerful women.

As a movie star, Eddie Murphy has the benefit of film studio costumers, set designers, actors, and financial backers to support his creative visions. But he didn't always have those things. He began with the same tool we are all born with: a powerful and empathic imagination.

Imagination Online and in Real Life

We may not all be as visionary as Eddie Murphy, but today girls and women can use our imaginations to create entire virtual lives through computer games such as the Sims (www.thesims.ea.com) and Second Life (www.secondlife.com). In the Sims, players simulate daily activities of virtual people who live in an online suburb where they sleep, eat, read, work, date, and do laundry. Launched in 2000, the Sims is the best-selling personal computer game in history. Its creator, Will Wright, refers to the Sims as a "virtual dollhouse." Sixty percent of the game's users are female.

Second Life, offering a similar experience to the Sims, launched online in 2003. In Second Life, you create an avatar, the virtual version of you, which can resemble you or look totally different, your choice. In Second Life, you can also live a daily existence online. Second Life's tagline is "Your world. Your imagination." It's an incredibly cool concept and it is no surprise to me that it is extremely popular. Well, guess what? "Your world. Your imagination" applies to the real world as well. Whatever you can imagine for yourself, you can achieve—right here in your first life.

One of my proudest personal achievements came out of my ability to imagine. In my thirties, I wanted to quit smoking (www.smokefree.gov). As you know if you have ever smoked, cigarettes become a part of your life and your persona. At the time I finally decided to quit, I couldn't talk on the phone without a cigarette. I worked at the Department of Health and smoked constantly (ironic, huh?). Because I worked for the department, I knew that legislation was about to launch saying that you could no longer smoke in office buildings. The first image I had was of lowering my phone out the window sixteen stories down to the street (these were the days before cell phones), so I could make my calls while smoking in front of the building! How could I talk on the phone or write anything without a cigarette in my hand?

But I knew I had to stop smoking. When I finally decided to quit, I would literally sit and think about what it would be like to do things without cigarettes. I didn't just think of the absence of cigarettes in my life. I imagined what would take their place. I wish I could tell you that I munched on carrot sticks to break the habit, but it was Junior Mints and LifeSavers (no wonder my back teeth are shot today). I would envision what I would do with my hands if they were not holding a cigarette and lighter. I imagined what my desk would look like without an ashtray and pack of cigarettes by the phone. I imagined how it would feel to walk into my apartment and not be hit with the smell of stale smoke.

This was before computers, games, virtual technology, or any other imagination stimulator. I imagined myself cigarette-free in my own mind. I had to see myself as a healthy nonsmoker before I could become one. This is what you must do for whatever you want to make happen in your life. If you want to win a seat on the local board of education, picture yourself at a podium giving campaign speeches. Envision your campaign Web site. Think about how it will feel to celebrate on election night. This is what many elite athletes do before a major competition: they sit and imagine themselves moving their bodies and executing their game plan perfectly. You can do this, too.

We all have endless opportunities to use our imaginations and then translate those visions into reality. Whether you do your imagining in your own head, on paper, on a computer, on a movie screen, or anywhere else, the important thing is to do it. Imagination is the first essential step toward taking action on behalf of your greatest dreams and desires. It also makes it possible for you to inspire others because you can imagine being in their shoes.

Imagination Is the First Step Toward Action

I invite you to use that power now. Use your imagination to envision what you want in your life; how you want your family, job, community, and world to be; what would make it all feel right and good and fulfilling. So many people ask me questions about how to find a new job, create a business, start a not-for-profit, or construct a new life. The answer begins with using your imagination.

Until you have some vision of where you're going, you can't figure out how to get there. You can't have the life you want until you can see it first. You may find that your imagination is difficult to access. As women, our minds are often saturated with all we don't want—the debt we want to get rid of, the pounds we want to lose, the jobs we want to quit. We seem almost embarrassed to ponder what it is we actually desire, but that is exactly what we need to do. Imagine more time with your family, earning more, seeing more of the world, giving back, having more fun, whatever you want. What would it look like to do the work you love? What would be your ideal state of health? What is your ideal relationship and family life? What products and services would be available in your community?

Now think beyond your immediate life. What would be the state of the environment? What programs would receive funding from the government? What would magazine advertisements look like? What opportunities would exist for women? What services would exist for children or the elderly? What would be possible? And how would all of this feel? Our imagination is a tool to help ourselves and to help others. As Harry Potter creator J. K. Rowling said in her 2008 commencement address at Harvard University, "Imagination is not only the uniquely human capacity to envision that which is now, and therefore the fount of all invention and innovation. In its arguably most transformative and revelatory capacity, it is the power that enables us to empathize with humans whose experiences we have never shared."

LaGuardia to Liberia: From the Ladies' Room to the Classroom

Here is what I want in my lifetime for all women and girls: Women at every decision-making table representing 50 percent or more of the decision makers. Equal access to water, food, health, safety, education, and work for all women and girls. Respect, dignity, and security for all people. Those are my values. These are the things that are important to me.

In the course of writing this book, the experience I had on the New York Thruway kept popping into my head. I thought of the long line to the ladies' room and imagined what I could do to change this situation that affects me and millions of women and girls in restrooms around the world. That line was an annoyance as well as a symbol of all the things we wait for without thinking we can change them. But I happen to believe we *can* change ladies' room lines—or anything else—if we try. To think through a campaign to do just that, I followed the steps laid out in this book.

First, I determined what success would look like. For a ladies' room campaign this was easy: it would mean no woman waiting in a ladies' room line. Then I turned to my best friend, Google, for help. I typed "ladies' room lines" into the search engine and started poking around. Almost immediately I found New York City's 2005 Women's Restroom Equity Bill, which requires public places to have a 2:1 ratio of women's rooms to men's rooms where only a 1:1 ratio had previously existed in building codes. Congresswoman Yvette Clarke, a New York City councilwoman at the time, proposed the legislation and built up support to pass the bill. Clarke is now a member of the U.S. House of Representatives. Within ten minutes I'd found an ally in Congress who "gets it." Cool.

I got excited, so I kept clicking. After about a minute more of searching I found Professor Mary Anne Case of the University of Chicago Law School. She is running an online toilet survey, asking men and women to talk about how long they wait, how long they take to go, and what kinds of stuff they wish that public bathrooms had available. Bingo: a friend in academia. Soon I come across even more people who are frustrated about waiting. My world quickly opened up to the blogosphere, where women are sharing hundreds of stories, jokes, and photos related to those endless restroom lines.

Next, I search a little deeper—this is really fun!—and find the American Restroom Association (www.american

restroom.org). They've just come out with a press release identifying restroom availability as a key public health issue and link to the World Toilet Organization (www.world toilet.org) and their annual World Toilet Summit. They offer the chance to sponsor a toilet in a needy community for five hundred bucks. What a great idea. I bookmark the page. Then I come across a 2005 *New York Times* article and I stop in my tracks. The article is about places where there are no ladies' rooms at all. I learn that one in ten school-age African girls either skips school during menstruation or drops out entirely because of lack of sanitation. There are no private places, even if there are latrines, for girls to wash when they have their periods and there is limited money for or availability of sanitary pads or tampons. "Even the women among the school's teachers say they have no choice but to use the thorny scrub, in plain sight of classrooms, as a toilet," the article says. I learn that lack of toilets is the reason for 10 percent of girls not going to school in Nepal.

Now I'm beyond irritated at our own waiting in restroom lines. I'm furious that girls aren't going to school because they have no place to go. The more I read, the more I want to do something about this. I begin to see the ladies' room campaign in the United States turning into a global campaign to help girls stay in school. Wouldn't it be amazing if public ladies' rooms featured huge posters with information about how to help improve sanitation around the world? I imagine a Web site people could visit on their smartphones that would enable them to donate money to these efforts.

Next I begin to think about potential partners who could provide funding and support. I come across a magazine advertisement from Tampax and Always announcing that the two brands are launching a program to help African girls stay in school by providing them with tampons and sanitary napkins. Procter and Gamble (P&G), the brands' parent company, is joining forces with HERO, an awareness building and fundraising initiative of the United Nations Association to launch the Protecting Futures program (www.protectingfutures.com), which will provide products and services to help keep girls healthy and in school.

I immediately search my contacts for people I know who might know someone related to this project. I have a friend who works at the United Nations, so I send him an e-mail. He happily agrees to a meeting in which I share my idea to use ladies' room lines in airports around the world to help girls and teachers with no bathrooms at all. He gets it immediately and quickly starts talking. He tells me about the United Nations Girls' Education Initiative (www.UNGEI.org), which has developed a program called Child Friendly Schools to address many issues, including washing areas in girls' bathrooms. I admit that it's pretty overwhelming to think about the fact that over 62 million girls around the world don't go to school. I asked my friend where he suggests we start.

"Liberia has a good approach," he replies.

Experts suggest that Liberia is the country with the greatest promise of solving the problem of sanitation for women and girls. Dr. Ellen Johnson-Sirleaf, the president of Liberia, is the world's first black female president and Africa's first elected female head of state. With the leadership of President Johnson-Sirleaf, Liberia has attracted the attention of UNICEF, the World Bank, and philanthropist George Soros, who have all committed to building child-friendly schools—with water—in all eight countries in Liberia. The total cost would be $73 million, which sounds daunting. But when you break it down, the cost amounts to $2,500 per school to make sure there is running water in each girls' bathroom.

It's all coming together. I have leads to big organizations with big resources. I see that much of the work has already been started. There are real dollar amounts to aim for. How quickly we've gone from wanting to change an irritation in our lives—waiting in ladies' room lines—to wanting to change the world for 62 million girls!

And that is exactly what can happen for you. Using your imagination and contacts is an incredibly powerful exercise. You may have a vision similar to mine or totally different. For some women, your ideal vision will encompass your family and immediate surroundings. For other women, your ideal vision may include wanting to change the world. Either way, the exercise of using your imagination muscle is the same. When you use your imagination, you stop waiting for life to come to you, and you grasp your power to have it your way. I know it. I've done it.

Exercise: Define Success on Your Terms

Now it's your turn. Write down exactly what it is that you would like to have in your life. What does your way look like? Perhaps it's changing jobs, improving your health, activating your community, deepening your spiritual practice, reducing your housework, getting a raise, getting a divorce, taking an extended maternity leave, retiring early, developing more friendships, anything. Start with the end in mind, and jot down some notes about your future:

_____

_____

_____

_____

_____

_____

_____

Your living arrangements:

_____

_____

_____

_____

Relationships:

_____

_____

_____

_____

_____

Work/career/calling:

_____

_____

_____

_____

_____

Health:

_____

_____

_____

Wealth:

_____

_____

_____

Spirituality:

_____

_____

_____

_____

_____

Tools to Activate Your Imagination

Now that you've seen the power of imagination and written down the beginnings of your vision, let's look at some specific tools that will help you access your imagination and make sure you are thinking as creatively and gloriously as possible.

1. Make Your Own Rules

Too many women think that success and happiness have to do with following rules—other people's rules—as opposed to making your own. Just as the system is more malleable than you think, rules are more flexible than you think. Yes, there are rules that you have to follow, like the Ten Commandments if you're Christian, the Golden Rule, the Koran, Murphy's law, the laws of Mother Nature and gravity, but the rest is up to you.

Go ahead right now and create your own rules, your own vision, any way you want. It's easiest to use an established document as a guideline for writing your own rules—for instance, you can write your own Ten Commandments or a personal Bill of Rights. My document of choice is the famous Proust Questionnaire, a nineteenth-century personality questionnaire—a party game at the time—made popular by the responses of the French writer Marcel Proust. Since Proust's time, the questionnaire has appeared in magazines (the back page of *Vanity Fair*) and television shows (James Lipton's *Inside the Actor's Studio*) as a way for interviewers to probe the lives and beliefs of celebrities. We all read these types of interviews with great interest and feel so curious about famous people's answers. This is probably because we compare their answers to our own.

So, forget about the celebrities and just record your own answers. The Proust Questionnaire is an excellent tool for probing your imagination and discovering important clues about what you want in life—what is important to you and what rules you want to live by.

The Proust Questionnaire

My answers appear below, because I've always wanted to answer the Proust Questionnaire! I hope you'll follow my lead and fill out the questionnaire in the exercise that follows.

What do you regard as the lowest depth of misery?
Confinement or restraints—physical and intellectual
Where would you like to live?
New York City, where I live
What is your idea of earthly happiness?
Riding bikes at the beach with my husband
Who are your favorite heroes and heroines of fiction?
Celie from The Color Purple *and Maya from* The Fifth Sacred Thing
Who are your favorite characters in history?
Sojourner Truth, Elizabeth Cady Stanton, Elizabeth I, Galileo
Who are your favorite heroines in real life?
My mother, Hillary Clinton, Judith Jamison, the women of Rwanda, Billie Jean King

Who are your heroes in real life?

My father, Nelson Mandela, Hamid Karzai, Barack Obama

Your favorite painter?

J.M.W. Turner and Mary Cassatt

Your favorite musician?

Mozart and Mary J. Blige

The quality you most admire in a man?

Authenticity

The quality you most admire in a woman?

Authenticity

Your favorite virtue?

Diligence

Your favorite occupation?

What I do: rabble-rouser, leader of women

What would you have liked to be?

A trapeze artist

Your most marked characteristic?

Confidence

What do you most value in your friends?

Acceptance

What is your dream of happiness?

Being on a beach holiday with my family

What to your mind would be the greatest of misfortunes?

Not being free

What would you like to be?

Exactly what I am

In what country would you like to live?

USA

What is your favorite color?

Red

Who are your favorite writers?

Rohinton Mistry, author of A Fine Balance, *and Alice Walker*

What are your favorite names?

Margolo, the name of the bird from Stuart Little

What is it you most dislike?

Inequality, discrimination

What natural gift would you most like to possess?

An ability to do acrobatics

How would you like to die?

In my sleep when I am over one hundred years old

What is your present state of mind?

Grateful, excited, accelerated, global

What is your motto?

"Knockers Up!"

EXERCISE: What's Your Answer?

Now you try! Fill in your own responses to the questions below.

What do you regard as the lowest depth of misery?

Where would you like to live?

What is your idea of earthly happiness?

Who are your favorite heroes and heroines of fiction?

Who are your favorite characters in history?

Who are your favorite heroines in real life?

Who are your heroes in real life?

Your favorite painter?

Your favorite musician?

The quality you most admire in a man?

The quality you most admire in a woman?

Your favorite virtue?

Your favorite occupation?

What would you have liked to be?

Your most marked characteristic?

What do you most value in your friends?

What is your dream of happiness?

What to your mind would be the greatest of misfortunes?

What would you like to be?

In what country would you like to live?

What is your favorite color?

Who are your favorite writers?

What are your favorite names?

What is it you most dislike?

What natural gift would you most like to possess?

How would you like to die?

What is your present state of mind?

What is your motto?

Did anything surprise you in your answers? Did any themes emerge? What can you learn from the people and characters you admire? What rules did they follow or not follow? There are often seeds of our desires in our answers to the above questions. Find yours and let your imagination run with the possibilities that arise from your new, personal set of rules.

Rewriting the rules is not a modern phenomenon. Elizabeth Cady Stanton did this in the late 1800s. A wife, mother, and member of polite society, Stanton used the tools of her day to imagine a different world for herself and for all women. In 1898, Stanton published her own version of the most well-read rule book of her day, and probably of all time: the Bible. You can't get much more audacious, imaginative, or creative than rewriting the Bible!

The Woman's Bible preface states, "The object is to revise only those texts and chapters directly referring to women, and those also in which women are made prominent by exclusion." And that is exactly what Stanton and her fellow authors did. They revised the Bible to be more relevant for, and respectful to, women. You can read the entire *The Woman's Bible* online. Simply go to http://books.google.com and type in "The Woman's Bible."

Stanton and her "revising committee" felt the need to rewrite the Bible because men kept evoking the Bible as a reason why women should not have the vote. Stanton thought the easiest solution was to simply rewrite the text they were citing. If that's not rewriting the rule book, I don't know what is!

2. Talk—A Lot

My natural instinct is to share every piece of valuable information I get. When I have an idea, I tell people. When I hear a good story, I share it. When I have a question, I ask it. When I learn something, I want to share it with others. In the case of Count Me In for Women's Economic Independence, instead of figuring out how to expand my own communications business, I created an organization that helps all women expand their businesses. In the case of this book, I wanted to share everything I've learned by stepping out of line in my life. Don't hoard what you know. Share it, and you'll learn even more. To expand your vision, start talking about it.

One of the main ways I have shared my vision is through the press. Because of my background in politics and communications, I always think about how an idea or campaign will play in the press and all media platforms: What would be the headline of the press release or the subject line of an e-mail? What's the sound bite? Even if you're not planning to write a press release about spending more time in nature or negotiating a flextime agreement with your boss, do think about your pitch—to the people in your life who can help you achieve your goals. When you step out of line, you create buzz—and that's a good thing. Buzz creates energy.

When you begin to share your imagination with other people—even tiny nuggets—it is amazing what synergies occur. Sharing your wildest imaginings can be exciting, but it is also the fastest way to make your vision come true. This is what happened in consciousness-raising groups in the 1960s and 1970s. This is what happened when Betty Friedan published *The Feminine Mystique* and ambitious, college-educated housewives around the country learned they weren't the only ones feeling frustrated mopping their kitchen floors and imagining different lives for them-selves. This is what happened when I started sharing my idea for Take Our Daughters to Work Day. This is what happens at every event for the Make Mine a Million $ Business program, when women business owners realize they are part of a growing movement of women imagining themselves as economically independent people.

Bill Dueease, president of the Coach Connection, a Make Mine a Million $ Business partner, captured this beautifully: "[Women in the Make Mine a Million $ Business community] want to spend focused and quality time together. They all want to share their experiences and successes with the mutual issues they have in common. I believe that the group of women owners you have now and certainly will have is—and will continue to be—the best source of information, perspectives, details, and support to the other women business owners. The Movement! The mutual sharing, discoveries, and support between them is priceless for both the givers and the receivers."

3. Study People You Admire—or Envy

Although it's certainly possible, it can be difficult to imagine yourself doing something you've never witnessed before. To expand your imagination and learn the steps to get where you want to go, watch other people.

There Is Rarely a Need to Reinvent the Wheel

Operate under the assumption that you are never the only one who wants the thing that you desire. Other people want it, too. And, if other people want what you want, they've probably taken some action that you can learn from.

In some cases, those "other people" may be historical figures or fictional characters. When I was on the verge of firing an employee a few years ago, I had an instructive moment while watching the television show *Commander in Chief,* in which Geena Davis played the president of the United States. In this particular episode, she fired her female attorney general for using torture. I was mesmerized and wanting to soak in every bit of it. I walked up to my television screen and sat down right in front of it, so I could catch every detail of her words, facial expressions, and body language. When I saw Geena Davis's character fire an employee with honesty, grace, and firmness, I could picture myself doing it in a much more confident way.

If you're having trouble thinking of people you admire, try this trick: make a list of people you envy. Instead of coveting what the other person has or does, use the envious feeling as information. Acknowledge what you want, and start working on getting it for yourself.

It may feel uncomfortable to access your feelings of envy, but a lot of what sparks your imagination is not beautiful. Envy is a perfectly good trigger for your imagination. See yourself in the shoes of the person you envy. Do you want to copy that person in some way, or just the outcome he or she achieved? Dissect the envy. Study it. See it, feel it, write it down. Use it to help you get what you want. There is plenty of almost everything to go around, so if someone else has a situation you want, you can probably have it too. Rather than thinking there is one finite pie with only eight pieces to go around, think about making more pies or a bigger pie, so there is more than enough to go around.

4. Take a Lesson from Men

We can learn a lot from men. They've done an excellent job of defining success, making their own rules, and creating the world according to their vision. Most men seem to instinctively know what it means to make their own rules. It is men, of course, who have historically defined concepts such as success, work, happiness, love, beauty, safety, and more. It's no secret that women have been living by the male vision of the world for centuries. What if women started to set the tone and rewrite these concepts?

There is an editing technique called interpretive paraphrasing that can help women to think differently. Instead of reworking a sentence that needs help, interpretive paraphrasing calls for forgetting the original sentence and starting it over from scratch to say what you mean in your own words. This is much more effective than trying to fix a broken sentence. Women need to do this sort of editing to our own lives. Forget everything that might hold you back—including traditionally male definitions of success and happiness—and just start envisioning the life you want.

5. Bust the Savior Fantasy

It is perfectly fine if your vision of the future looks nothing like your current life. However, it is not okay if your vision looks like a fairy tale. If you are dreaming of finding a mate, don't fantasize about Prince Charming riding up on his white horse.

Instead, imagine your online dating profile and all of the e-mail responses you will receive. If you are dreaming of losing weight, don't fantasize about the pounds magically melting away. Instead, imagine yourself eating delicious, healthy meals and going for long walks in nature or around your neighborhood with a good friend. If you want more time in your day, don't wish for the little rat from *Ratatouille* to magically appear in your kitchen to cook dinner for your kids. Instead, imagine yourself having fun with your kids while putting together meals at Dinner Helpers (www.dinnerhelpers.com), a business that offers fresh ingredients and meal prep stations for you to assemble several days' meals at a time before bringing them home to cook.

One of the many confusing stories of my childhood is the famous tale of the actress Lana Turner being discovered in a drugstore when she was fifteen. As a child, I thought that was a glamorous story—that Lana, known back then as Judy, had walked into the Schwab's Drugstore on Sunset Boulevard for a Coke and walked out that day on her way to stardom. (According to Lana Turner's official Web site, she wasn't actually at a Schwab's Drugstore, but the Top Hat Café, a shop across the street from Hollywood High.) She was discovered by the publisher of the *Hollywood Reporter,* who introduced her to an agent and director. The legend was born. My Aunt Connie—the one who promised chubby childhood me a new wardrobe at age eleven if I lost thirty pounds—often told me the Lana Turner story. She thought it would inspire me to lose weight so that I, too, could be discovered!

Lana Turner may be from another era, but we have a contemporary discovery story thanks to model Kate Moss. Her legend involves being discovered at age fourteen by a famous modeling agent while she was preparing to board a flight at New York's JFK airport.

Bust Your Savior Fantasy

Are you holding on to a fairy-tale fantasy of being discovered, recognized, called up, picked out? If so, drop it right now. Instead, make a list of what you want to be discovered, recognized, called up or picked out for and start acting on it yourself.

Using your imagination and living your ideal life is not about luck or fantasy. It is about showing up and auditioning, like you would for *American Idol*. Or, it is about losing on *American Idol* like actress and singer Jennifer Hudson and deciding to pursue a career—and win an Oscar!—anyway. It is about launching a business because you know you have a good idea. It is about asking for a raise or promotion instead of sitting around hoping to be noticed for your accomplishments. It is about taking action and being on your own team. Stepping out of line means dropping the myth that someone will find you and magically

transform your life. You've already found that champion—
it's you.

6. Shake Up Your Routine

Another way to activate your imagination is to get out
of your regular routine and expand your horizons. Start
seeing new and different people, neighborhoods, stores,
products, scenery, and images so you can imagine achieving new and different goals. For instance, think about
what you read on a regular basis—newspapers, Web pages,
magazines, blogs, books, everything. To keep my imagination constantly energized, I read everything I can get my
hands on. You name it, I read it. From *GQ* to *Gourmet* to
Ebony to *Star* to *The Economist,* I constantly try to expose
myself to different viewpoints, people, ideas, and visions
of the world. If you only read publications that agree with
your viewpoint and match your lifestyle, how can you picture anything different? Read anything and everything you
can (doctors' offices and airports are great for this), then
let your imagination take it all in.

Do the same with your actions. Whether you are walking or driving or taking the bus, alter your normal route
once in a while and see what you find. Stop into a new
store, walk your dog at a different park, or browse a random aisle of the library or video store. Get your children or
grandchildren to show you their favorite Web sites and
video games. Sometimes I imagine things when I'm just
sitting in a chair, staring into space. But, more likely, I
imagine while I am walking around, surfing at my com-

puter, taking a spin class, or watching a TV channel I've never seen before. You can jumpstart your imagination by feeding your brain different data than it normally receives.

7. Search Deep in Yourself

"Searching in yourself" may sound a little vague, but it isn't. Searching inside yourself means exploring your innate interests and desires. These could be lifelong passions or relatively new desires based on your current circumstances. Have confidence that your preferences will lead you to the life you want. Sometimes we don't even realize the wealth of information and ideas we have subconsciously surrounded ourselves with. Be a detective in your own life—in your home, in your mind, in your body, and in the hidden places in all of these. Here are some suggestions for searching inside your current life for the seeds of your future life.

- Scan your home. What is your favorite room in the house, the one where you feel most comfortable and happy? (If your favorite room is the kitchen, maybe you want to host more dinner parties, share more recipes, write a cookbook, focus more on nutrition, redesign that room.) What section of the newspaper do you read first? I scan the front page and then go right to the obituaries. I love the life stories even if very few women end up on that page. If you read the book reviews first, you might want to start a book club or take a writing class or spend more time reading to your kids. What are your favorite clothes to wear? I always have a current favorite item that I wear and wear. I remember reading Mother Teresa's obit where it said her earthly possessions were three blue saris and a prayer book. What a great way to eliminate figuring out what you are going to wear every day. The things you already do and have and feel provide a good indication of what you already enjoy or what you want to change.

- Think about your ideal "third place." Think about where you would most like to be when you are not at home or at work (however you define your work, including taking care of your home or children). What would be your "transition" or "third" place? For me, my ideal third place is a park where I can exercise, ride bikes, appreciate flowers, and have conversations while walking. For some people, their third place is Starbucks or a bar. What is yours? Imagine what it would feel like to spend more time in this place.

- Browse through a university or community college course book. Circle any classes that appeal to you, even if you don't know why. Those topics might be an indication of where your interests and desires lie. Then, sign up for the class that sounds most appealing. If you don't have time to attend classes, check out online learning programs, such as the University of Phoenix (www.phoenix.edu), Gotham Writers' Workshop (www.writingclasses.com), and the Learning Annex (www.learningannex.com). Education is a wonderful way to activate and feed your imagination.

• Spend an hour playing on Google or another search engine. Type in any terms that appeal to you—think of it as virtual word association. Start typing word combinations that are meaningful to you, and see what comes up in the search results. You can try anything:

  • Acting lessons + Miami
  • Organic cooking + Kids + Seattle
  • Art + Engineering + Women
  • Dogs + Knitting + Traveling
  • Sanitation + Girls + Education

  Just search on your interests and see what comes up. Trust that whatever you type will lead you somewhere. Don't hold back just because you don't know a specific Web site address or how to spell something. Just type! Google will put it all together with you. And, who knows—by mistyping you may find something even more interesting.

8. Whenever You Feel Overwhelmed, Keep Imagining

It may seem counterintuitive, but sometimes it is easier to think bigger rather than smaller. How far could your vision of success and fulfillment spread? Focusing on self-improvement is wonderful, but what truly transforms you is when your goals and accomplishments take you out of yourself. Let your imagination grow to include the contribution you want to make to the world. As you have already seen in the stories of other women, by living life on your terms you demonstrate to other women that they can live life on their own terms too.

There's a Reason It's Called Activating Your Imagination
As these eight tools make clear, using your imagination is an active pursuit. It requires thinking, reading, talking, learning, exploring, and moving around. Imagination leads to action, and it also *requires* action.

Making the Private Public

Private pain turned into public action at the Gathering of Remembrance and Renewal in 1991, an event designed to heighten awareness in the tenth year of the AIDS epidemic. Imagination was a key ingredient of planning the event and making sure the commemoration made a difference in people's lives.

One of the biggest lessons I learned from working to heighten the awareness about AIDS is the vital importance of speaking out about private issues that have traditionally been hidden from "polite" public conversation. Even after ten years in the public consciousness, AIDS deaths were still considered a private affair. At one of my first meetings with the Gay Men's Health Crisis (GMHC, www.gmhc.org), I suggested that we use the tenth anniversary event to honor the 130,000 people who had died. I received unanimous looks of dismay.

"We don't use the D word here," the chairman of the board told me.

That, I thought, was the problem.

In order to have a real impact, the thousands of AIDS deaths needed to register in the public imagination. But how? There were only so many times and ways you could scare people about the state of the world or their health.

This project called for sensitivity, creativity, and, of course, imagination. My spark of insight came from reading books about the Day of the Dead in Mexico and the city of Varanasi in India, on the Ganges River. In Mexico, whole families spend the day at the cemetery honoring and visiting with their departed ancestors in the beginning of November. Graves are cleaned and decorated and the departed person's favorite food is eaten around the grave. At Varanasi, Hindus come together to take ritual baths, worship their gods, and burn their dead on funeral pyres that float on the river. Thinking of this public confluence of death, celebration, prayer, and offerings, I imagined an AIDS memorial service that did the same thing—placed the living and dead in the same space. The largest public space I could think of was the church of St. John the Divine (www.stjohndivine.org)—the largest cathedral in the world, two football fields long—on the Upper West Side of Manhattan.

In my imaginings about the event, the use of light was paramount. I worked with the head of production at the church to turn this somewhat hazy vision into reality. He devised a method for placing plastic gels over spotlights to produce a twinkling, glowing effect. During the memorial, we projected 130,000 stars of light on the vaulted ceiling of St. John, each representing a person who had died from AIDS. It was one thing to read the words: 130,000 have died. It was quite another to see a dense cluster of stars amassed on the magnificent domed ceiling and realize that each represented a human story that had been halted by this disease.

The Gathering of Remembrance and Renewal took place on November 22, 1991. It really did feel like the living and the dead were together in the same room— mourning and celebrating, educating and warning. The private, wrenching tragedy of personal loss was made vividly public so that everyone could feel, hear, and see the same need. The AIDS crisis could not be addressed if it remained a private issue, "in the dark." And the magical effect of light in the church of St. John the Divine all started with a spark of imagination.

How My Imagination Changed My Life, Part I: Losing My Way

Working to move the issue of AIDS from the private to the public sphere helped me to step out of line and stand out more in my own life. It was that event that drew the attention of the Ms. Foundation and prompted them to ask me for ideas to bring the issue of girls' self-esteem from the private to the public. I stood out because I made the private public.

In addition to using my imagination to create major campaigns and quit smoking, I have used this incredible tool to solve many other challenges. In fact, I credit my imagination with launching the time of greatest positive change in my life so far. This story begins during a historic, thrilling moment in 1984, about a decade before the Gathering of Remembrance and Renewal and Take Our Daughters to Work Day. I was at the Moscone Convention Center in San Francisco the day when Walter Mondale introduced Geraldine Ferraro as his vice presidential running mate. The moment the announcement occurred, almost every woman in the room rushed to the phones in the scheduling office at the convention center to call her mother. I didn't have to make a call because I was there with mine. She was a delegate to the Democratic Convention from New Jersey—male delegates had given women alternates their floor passes for the occasion. I have a photo of the two of us, standing on chairs, waving flags and crying, two generations of Merlino women. All around us, there was weeping and great joy, astonishment that this had finally happened. At last women would be valued as equals in the most powerful place in the world—the White House.

I had not seen much of my parents during that year because I was working on the Mondale campaign, doing scheduling and advance work. At the time of Ferraro's nomination, I'd just spent a challenging, exhausting six months entrenched in a testosterone-saturated environment where all the big decisions were made by men. It felt like unless you were sleeping with one of the guys in the upper reaches of the Democratic Party organization, you weren't included in any of the decision-making meetings. Watching the men gather all the information from us women then retreat to a room and shut us out was so debilitating.

Still, I found presidential politics fast paced and relentless—a whirl of nonstop action and strategizing—like a combat zone or an emergency room. Working with a diverse, high-powered group of people from across the country, I had the heady sense that we were in the midst of making history, that I was actually watching how power was won and lost.

The day of the official Ferraro nomination, the convention hall had an electric feeling. A powerful roar rose up from the crowd as Ferraro approached the platform. When she reached the podium she spoke about her immigrant heritage. Then she said, "Tonight, the daughter of a woman whose highest goal was a future for her children talks to our nation's oldest party about a future for us all."

As an Italian American myself, I felt proud. Watching

someone in my own image standing on a stage saying she is ready to lead the country sent shivers of joy and recognition from the top of my head down my back and neck. Geraldine Ferraro was stepping way out of line, and if she could, then millions of other women and I could, too.

Gloria Steinem recounts a story how a few days after the nomination, a young black jogger recognized her as he ran by. He smiled and called out, "Isn't it great? Now you can be president."

And she yelled back, "No, you can be president."

The man smiled and said, "Now any of us can be president."

Such was the impact, the sense of hope and momentousness that surrounded the occasion.

As we all know, Geraldine Ferraro did not end up a heartbeat away from the Oval Office. A woman's vote failed to materialize in 1984. Fifty-five percent of women who voted cast their ballot for Reagan/Bush. Was it Ferraro's tax problem with her husband? Was it simply impossible for Walter Mondale to beat Ronald Reagan? Was it because George H. W. Bush said he had "kicked a little ass" after their vice presidential debate? We'll never know.

What I do know is that the time following the Mondale/Ferraro campaign was one of the most difficult, confusing periods of my life. I was in my mid-to-late thirties and had just worked on the most exciting job of my life thus far. I had seen things that were really big—how the country works, massive power, and high-stakes failure. After Mondale and Ferraro lost, I headed back to New York with no idea what to do next. I began working for the Department of Health, researching issues like AIDS (which wasn't even called AIDS yet), long-term care insurance, and day-care centers for people with Alzheimer's disease. I was single, living alone, and all I did was work.

Eventually, in 1986, I began to work on New York governor Mario Cuomo's potential reelection campaign, but I wasn't happy this time. I didn't feel challenged anymore. I felt stuck in the "family business" of my father's world—politics and state government. Everything in politics was about building the success of somebody else. It was all about being a good soldier and keeping your mouth shut and doing what you were told. And, boy, was it sexist. Anyone who watches political news coverage today can see that very little has changed in this world. National politics is the ultimate glass ceiling for women, even if Hillary Clinton and her supporters put 18 million cracks in it, as Clinton proclaimed in her June 2008 primary concession speech. I can't tell you how many times a young guy ten years my junior would join the campaign and start telling me what to do.

At that point, I just didn't know what else to do. When you have worked in politics, joining a national campaign is a way of tossing your cards up in the air and seeing where they land. It offers a chance to reconnect with a whole lot of fascinating, powerful people. Maybe you'll end up in the administration or get a job offer with someone after the campaign. It is a bit like going to graduate school. It's also a lot like waiting.

I knew I wanted a full life. I didn't want to continue working all the time, but at that point I didn't want to get married or raise a family either. I wanted something different. But when I looked around me, I didn't see any models for the kind of life I wanted to lead as a woman. So, in order to create the kind of life I wanted—a life of professional satisfaction, personal fulfillment, health, love, community, and success—I had to use my imagination and get a lot of help.

How My Imagination Changed My Life, Part II: Imagining an OrganiFloraSpaXercise-atorium

I can't really explain why, but when I was depressed, frustrated, and unsure of my direction, my natural instinct was to use my imagination. Perhaps because I didn't like my outer world, I retreated into the inner world of my creative mind. What happened was amazing. I found myself imagining big—really big.

In the opening scenes of *Coming to America*, Eddie Murphy imagined a kingdom where he has access to everything a young man could possibly desire. Well, during my deep funk following the Mondale campaign, I began to imagine a place where I would have access to everything a single thirty-something Manhattan woman would desire. I started to imagine a place I can only describe as an OrganiFloraSpaXercise-atorium.

It began as a fun daydream and soon grew into a serious

creative pursuit. I spent hours upon hours envisioning a place where I and other women like me would stop in on the way to work or home from work—a full-service "third place." It would be full of plants, lovely aromas, people happy to support you, and lots of activity and joy. My imagination was sparked by a place I had visited in London when I was a student, called the Sanctuary. I suppose you could describe the Sanctuary as an early spa—it had a heated pool, steam rooms, saunas, massages, and facials. It was an oasis, and not that expensive.

I imagined the OrganiFloraSpaXercise-atorium as a place that would offer beauty and pampering, but also practical services and community. It would be welcoming and accepting, a true neighborhood hub, designed to support women, both married and single, and their families (men would certainly be welcome) in all aspects of their lives. It would combine the civic cohesiveness of an earlier social era—the 1940s and 1950s, when my father sat in the Italian social clubs of Trenton, drank espresso, and played cards with his friends—with the social and technological realities of the 1980s.

The OrganiFloraSpaXercise-atorium would recognize and encourage the many facets that encompass a woman's nature: her desire to work and make money, her needs as a social creature, nurturer, and friend. It wouldn't deny or degrade the responsibilities women have or their desire to be wives or mothers. Instead, it would collectively help us deal with these multiple roles. Entering it would be like slipping into an oasis from the crowded city, a sanctuary of indoor fountains, tropical plants, and soothing music. Everyone who entered would be asked to contribute what she or he is gifted at and to partake of what they need. Because of this, people would feel useful and united in a purpose larger than each of them.

I imagined that each facet of a person's life would be represented on a different floor of the building. The first floor would be dedicated to the body, with a state-of-the-art gym facility, spas and a swimming pool, as well as martial arts and yoga classes, hair and nail salons, and massage rooms. The domestic second floor would be a bustling center for all the labor that women have traditionally shouldered, with a laundry, dry cleaner, and a pharmacy. A third-floor tech center would offer high-tech computer systems and other necessities so people could conduct work outside their fluorescent-lit offices. Day care and elder care would be combined on the fourth floor, where multiple generations would be encouraged to exchange their gifts and contribute to each other's lives. And finally, there would be a floor dedicated to fresh organic food that could be eaten in, taken out, or assembled and prepared for later cooking at home.

I imagined the OrganiFloraSpaXercise-atorium to be the exact kind of place I wanted to have as a single woman. It was a place I wish my mother had had when she was struggling to work, raise five kids, and serve dinner each night. It was a place I wish my siblings and I had had during my father's final illness at that time, when it took the time and resources of five of his adult children to navigate a complex, alienating medical bureaucracy. It was a place I wanted young girls to grow up with. For months, I sketched pictures of its various rooms and talked about it with friends. I made lists of how far-reaching its impact could be.

How My Imagination Changed My Life, Part III: Turning Imagination into Action

Amazingly, as I started to imagine the OrganiFlora-SpaXercise-atorium, my depression and frustration began to evaporate. Even though I was still unhappy at my day job, I started to see possibilities for something better. My imagining about the OrganiFloraSpaXercise-atorium began as a fantasy, but as you'll see, it grew into very real—and very wonderful—results.

At first, I started to make notes about how I would create this amazing place. I thought about the people I knew in government who might take this on as a cause. I researched zoning laws. I tried to find examples in other countries or cities that might be helpful. As I dug deeper and deeper into the reality of actually building and managing an OrganiFloraSpaXercise-atorium, my interest flagged. I slowly realized that what I loved was imagining the idea, planning it and talking about it, not necessarily developing architectural plans and overseeing construction.

This increasing self-knowledge of what I loved to do coincided with an increasing desire to leave my state government job. It also coincided with a total lack of interest in any job listings I found that were suited to my political and government experience.

Around that time, my dear friend Tom Blatner was also working in a job in state government that kept getting worse, not better. He got fired and started up his own consultancy. Bingo—a role model! We talked about going into business together. But when Tom told me the name of his business was Blatner & Associates, I knew I would be starting something of my own. I didn't want to be an invisible associate.

And so, although I did not pursue the OrganiFlora-SpaXercise-atorium, my imaginings about that place led me to start my own business, which I did in 1988. To this day, I can say that starting a business is the most liberating thing I've ever done. I found it thrilling to be an entrepreneur and be in control of my own work schedule and income. I ran the business out of my personal checkbook for the first few years and remember getting my first business checks in 1993. I made business cards on my dot matrix printer. I named the business Strategy Communication Action, Ltd. (SCA), a name I chose on the way to the bank to get my business checks.

My company's very first contract was with the city of Camden, New Jersey. Our job was to devise a way to pull together all the different city entities that handled at-risk children and help them coordinate efforts. Desperately ill children as young as six years old were attempting suicide due to lack of care. We called the initiative "The Buck Stops Here" and negotiated an agreement from all parties that they would stop passing the kids around from agency to agency. The next year, we organized a homeless march from New York to Washington, D.C. In 1990 we developed the strategic communications plan for the twentieth anniversary of the Earth Day concert in Central Park, which attracted almost 1 million people. After that we handled events for Nelson Mandela and Mikhail Gorbachev.

Every project called for the exact skills and passion I had used to imagine the OrganiFloraSpaXercise-atorium. I felt successful and happy because I was getting great work and people were responding to it, but the feeling of success was deeper than that. Having my own business doing what I loved gave me energy. Nothing felt hard. I didn't feel depressed or frustrated anymore. By creating my own business, I created my ideal work environment with great clients and colleagues. And I got to work in my pajamas like Hugh Hefner. Over the next few years, I had life, love, and work my way: I grew the business, began exercising regularly, created Take Our Daughters to Work Day, and met and married my husband. Without a doubt, I credit this period of huge personal and professional growth to the work I did in therapy and to stretching my imagination. That process clarified my values, my talents, my passions, and my desires. It helped me become completely clear about my way to live and make a difference in the world.

ORGANIFLORASPAXERCISE-ATORIUMS
DO EXIST! (SORT OF)

I did not choose to pursue the creation of an OrganiFloraSpaXercise-atorium. However, as often is the case, I wasn't the only person imagining a third place for health, support, fun, creativity, and community.

Look around and you'll see the spa craze, an explosion of gourmet food stores like Trader Joe's and Whole Foods and gyms—even ones specifically for women—in every other strip mall and city neighborhood. Many residential housing complexes now feature dry cleaning and concierge services, gyms, pools, party rooms, and babysitting services. A new woman-owned business called Dinner Helpers (www.dinnerhelpers.com) now exists where you arrive at one of their locations and compile meals at prep stations where the shopping, chopping, and measuring have been done for you. You just assemble a week's worth of meals and take them home to cook. Today's elder-care facilities offer mentoring between kids and elderly residents. Many hotels and spas now offer special packages for single women and their friends or their pets. Various "mega-churches" (defined as non-Catholic churches with at least two thousand members) around the country now include onsite day care, coffee shops, magazines, financial literacy courses, and discussion groups. My brother and sister-in-law in Colorado take their kids to a family recreation center that has a pool, waterslide, a gym, an indoor track, a drop-in child-care center, and lots of other families to socialize with. We may not call any of these places an OrganiFloraSpaXercise-atorium, but the services and spirit are similar to my original vision.

EXERCISE: Imagining Your Version of an OrganiFloraSpaXercise-atorium

How can you visualize something like an OrganiFlora-SpaXercise-atorium and use that vision as a catalyst for change? The process involves all of the tools of imagination we've discussed. Start exploring places, publications, people, and products that you've never explored before. One idea sparks another idea, and then another, and then another. Just take the first step and see where it takes your imagination.

Of course, there is an element of whimsy to this process as well—enjoy it! It reminds me of when I broke my foot a few years ago. I had to decide what things I needed around me, within arm's reach, since I couldn't walk around easily at all. This is a great exercise to try: What "stuff" (things, people, feelings, etc.) do you need within arm's reach in your life? Just start conjuring an image of everything you could ever want or need to have around you. What would you create? What do you need in your life to make it work?

"Checking" Your Imagination: A Values Exercise

How did I know that I didn't want to dedicate my life to actually building an OrganiFloraSpaXercise-atorium? Essentially, I did a gut check. It just didn't feel right or fulfilling to become a building manager. My heart wasn't in that work. My values were aligned with the idea of the OrganiFloraSpaXercise-atorium, but not with the act of building it. This is how I came to create a strategic communications company instead.

Align Your Imagination with Your Values

To turn imagination into real action in your life, you must make sure that the things you imagine are in line with your personal values and passions. There are many ways to get what you want, but the most fulfilling path is the path that is ethical, authentic, and deeply meaningful to you.

What are your core reasons for being? Why do you get up in the morning? It's important to take time and define exactly why you want to live your life the way you do. In other words, what values are driving your vision? My values are very clear to me: freedom, creativity, enterprise, community, and love of my family. Freedom allows me the time and money to be with my family. Creativity is what keeps me fascinated and makes work fun for me. I keep these values top-of-mind when I think about new campaigns to pursue, when I interview employees to work for my organization, when I make decisions about what opportunities to pursue, and when I make daily decisions about how to spend my time.

No matter how big your vision expands, you must always come back to your core reasons for being—this is what ultimately separates imagination from fantasy.

EXERCISE: Determine Your Top Five Values

Your values help you to determine the people, opportunities, resources, and ideas that will ultimately lead to a life you desire. Your values are what you want. There is a Web site that lists over three hundred values. Values are completely personal and should not be determined by anyone but you. Getting clear about your values serves as a check that helps you decide which of your many visions is really worth pursuing.

What are your core values? Below is a list to spark your thinking:

Accomplishment	Independence
Adventure	Influence
Altruism	Learning
Beauty	Loyalty
Bravery	Optimism
Curiosity	Peace
Education	Respect

Environmental responsibility	Security
Faith	Self-discovery
Financial success	Status
Helping others	Truth
Rigor	Wealth
Risk-taking	Worldliness

Take a moment to list the top five values that are most important to you:

1.

2.

3.

4.

5.

Once you have some clarity around your core values, ask yourself if those values are connected to your vision of what you want in your life. If not, perhaps you need to search deeper for your vision and change direction. This values check helps to make sure your imagination is truly in line with what you want. Defining your values may lead your life in unexpected directions.

How Clarifying Your Values
Can Change Your Life

The combination of imagination and values is a forceful, powerful, magical mixture. Creating this synergy led my dear friend Isisara Bey to a surprising and wonderful new direction in her life.

Isisara and I went to college together and we reconnected when I was looking for corporate sponsors for the YWCA Week Without Violence. At the time she handled philanthropy for Sony. During one of our meetings about the event, the subject of revenge came up.

"You know, it really doesn't work," Isisara said quietly.

I asked what made her say that.

"I went to the trial of the man who murdered my husband. It didn't work for me."

I was shocked. I'd had no idea that Isisara's husband had been murdered. It happened in 1987 when she was living in Baltimore. Her husband had fallen in with drugs and a bad crowd. He had actually moved out of their home several months before he was killed. The murder was an act of jealousy and rage by a man who was dating the same woman as Isisara's husband. The man was arrested and went to trial.

"I was there when the verdict was announced. My husband had been the leader in his family. Everybody seemed to fall apart afterwards. I was determined that his murder was not going to ruin me.

"After my husband died, I realized that I made some decisions about marriage and children. He and I didn't have kids, and I thought maybe it wasn't supposed to happen. I was in my late thirties and felt that I was going to live life as a single person. I didn't think anything was missing. At one point I took a personal development class in which we did a process called stage work. We would all sit in a circle and one person would sit opposite the facilitator in a director's chair. It took a lot of courage to sit in that chair—it had a way of bringing up stuff.

"I volunteered to sit in the chair and I started talking about relationships. The facilitator asked me, 'What would be your optimal relationship?'

"As I began to really think about and describe my optimal relationship, I started having these rushes like I was on acid. I felt high and giddy and giggly! I couldn't believe what it felt like—and what reaction I got—from being authentic and passionate and confident and real. I was totally in line with myself.

"I made a vow that I would not be part of any relationships that were not exactly what I wanted."

Two weeks later, Isisara received a phone call from a friend who worked at Harlem Hospital children's unit. The friend told her that a UN Peacekeeper from Ghana had had a relationship while stationed in Cambodia with a Khmer woman that had produced a beautiful baby girl. When he left the country the child was shunned and was now up for adoption.

"I knew instantly that this was what I wanted," says Isisara. "I realized that in that chair in class I had never specified that my optimal relationship would be with a man!" She immediately emptied her savings account and flew to Cambodia to adopt the child, Makara, her daughter, who is now fourteen years old.

There are so many beautiful lessons from this story. When Isisara found herself in a situation she didn't want, she used her imagination to see a better life. Clarifying her values then helped Isisara attract the kind of opportunities that she wanted and needed, guiding her to the opportunity for an ideal—although surprising—love relationship. And, once Isisara became totally clear on what her deepest values were, she was able to easily identify and take action on an opportunity that fit with those values.

Even when you feel 100 percent clear on your values, how can you know that you are making the right decision for your future? You can't ever know anything for certain, so the best you can do is trust your instincts, as Isisara did when she jumped on a plane to Cambodia to adopt her daughter.

Margery Miller, the first executive coach for the Make Mine a Million $ Business program, puts it this way:

"Through my years of coaching and consulting I have heard the same thing from people—when they listen to their inner voice and follow it, they succeed; when they ignore it and do what they think they 'should do' for whatever reason, it leads them astray and clouds their focus. Please remember that you are your best guide."

Clarify Your Values

As you define your life, take time to define why you want to live your life a certain way—what values are most important to you. Then keep these values top-of-mind when deciding how to spend your time, resources, and energy. While you can achieve anything you imagine, a values check will confirm that you are pursuing a vision of the future that will really make you satisfied and fulfilled.

Imagining Power: The Women of Rwanda

It is hard to overemphasize the power of imagination to change lives. The final example I'll share is the story of the women of Rwanda and what they did after the horrific genocide in their country. It's the story of an entire society of women using their collective powers of imagination and affirming their deepest values to find a new way of living.

In 2004 I attended an event hosted by Vital Voices (www.vitalvoices.org), a nonprofit organization founded by Hillary Clinton when she was first lady, that builds leadership skills in women around the globe. There was a woman onstage representing a women's organization in Rwanda. As she began to tell her story, I was thunderstruck. She announced that Rwanda sat atop the world rankings of women in national parliaments, with 49 percent of representation compared to a world average of only 15.1 percent. Less than fifteen years after the staggering genocide of 1994, when Rwandan women suffered death, humiliation, persecution, and rape during a hundred-day massacre that left more than 800,000 people dead, they were now leaders in governance and civil society.

This did not occur simply because there were so few men left in the country. Rwandan women lobbied heavily, helped to draft the new constitution, and developed voting guidelines that guaranteed seats for women candidates. They were also able to push for the creation of a government ministry of women's affairs to promote policies in favor of women's interests. (See www.un.org.) Beyond transforming government, Rwandan women took on the responsibility of raising orphaned children. According to Vital Voices, when the dust settled from the horrific genocide and half a million children were orphaned, the women decided that children were their highest priority. They committed to each take one child. Here was a moment in time where you had thousands upon thousands of women butchered, bleeding, and raped. Somehow the survivors all came to a similar conclusion: They wanted to live, and they had to live differently in order to take care of themselves and the children who were left. Rwandan women stepped into their power and used their imaginations to save their country's future.

We shouldn't have to watch 800,000 people be murdered to understand that we are all responsible for ourselves. You cannot turn your safety over to someone else, not even your government. To deal with fear and create a safe environment, you must take responsibility for your own by being engaged in civil society.

What can you learn from Rwanda? Does it take a devastating catastrophe for women to use our power? When a woman loses a job, a house, a husband, or a child, she too has to decide that no one is coming to save her. The greatest myth going is that anyone is going to rescue us besides us.

That is what we can learn from Rwanda: power comes from inside, and we all have access to it. As long as we are willing to give power up and believe in an exchange that by not being fiercely for ourselves, we will somehow be rewarded—that none of this will happen to us, that we will be safe—we are vulnerable. Every one of those women in Rwanda believed that her husband, boss, or pastor would save her. But they didn't. It's all an illusion. To go on, women in Rwanda needed to see themselves as powerful. And that is exactly what they did.

These facts and stories speak to the power, depth, and empathic force of imagination. It is a tool that can be accessed by anyone and applied in countless ways. Imagination is a vital force that can transform lives, transform communities, and truly transform the world. It can guide us to achieve our biggest and boldest dreams and, as you'll see in the next chapter, help us to solve our most difficult and frustrating challenges.

GAINING FROM COMPLAINING

People often ask me how they will "know" how to live the lives they want and where and when to take action to reach their goals. As you've seen in the imagination exercises, one way to access your desires is to ask, What makes me feel most engaged? This is an indication of what career and personal activities will be satisfying to you.

However, another question, What makes me mad?, also stirs your imagination and provides insight into what pursuits will be satisfying. What bothers you so much that you really want to change it? What problems or frustrations do you want to shine a light on so solutions can be found? What makes you passionate in a positive or a negative way? Looking to your passion—whether it warms your heart or makes your blood boil—provides clues to what life path you will find fulfilling. I've named this practice "gaining from complaining."

Gaining from complaining means exercising your right to do something about things that bother you—whether those things are small daily irritants or major life-and-death issues (both of which we'll explore in this chapter). Gaining from complaining is about not waiting for problems to change or stop or go away. Gaining from complaining is another tool you can use to step out of line and live the life you desire. Through gaining from complaining, you can identify your passion, find engagement, and feel the satisfaction that comes from addressing your frustrations.

Let's look at some examples from projects I've worked on and from other women who have used their frustration to change their lives—and often the lives of other women as well. Some of these complaints were public and some were private, but all of them had profound results.

Gaining from Complaining About Violence

In 1994, two hundred girls gathered for lunch under the giant star magnolia trees on the South Lawn of the White House. They were greeted by President Bill Clinton, Vice President Al Gore, First Lady Hillary Clinton, Tipper Gore, and many VIPs from the media, business, and non-profit worlds. The event, which honored the second year of Take Our Daughters to Work Day, was dedicated to Laquanda Edwards, a twelve-year-old girl who was killed by a sniper's bullet as she stepped out of her apartment at Chicago's Cabrini Green housing project.

It was a poignant day. For at the same time in the early

1990s that we were making girls more visible in the world, and even at the White House, through Take Our Daughters to Work Day, too many children were being gunned down in drive-by shootings and gang violence. Crack cocaine was destroying lives and entire communities. Guns were everywhere, even in kids' lockers at school.

Organizations like the YWCA, which had actively participated in the success of Take Our Daughters to Work Day, wanted to do something about it. Founded over 160 years ago in part to provide women with a safe place to go when they traveled alone, in the 1990s, the challenge of creating safe places for women had reached crisis proportions. YWCAs across the country found themselves doing rape crisis counseling, running domestic violence shelters, teaching child abuse prevention, and holding gang negotiations.

A short time after the first Take Our Daughters to Work Day, Dr. Prema Mathai Davis, the new national leader of the YWCA of the USA, followed me into the ladies' room at a conference and asked me if I could create a campaign for the YWCA that would have a similar impact.

This led to the creation of the YWCA Week Without Violence, which started October 15–21, 1995, and continued for five years.

Just as Take Our Daughters to Work Day grew out of a movement to make girls more visible in public, specifically in the workplace, the YWCA Week Without Violence grew out of private suffering moving into the public spotlight. In 1992, photographer Donna Ferrato's shocking book on domestic violence, *Living with the Enemy,* showed images most people had never seen in public. Then, in June 1994, O. J. Simpson's wife Nicole Brown Simpson was murdered, leading to not only the biggest media circus the world had ever seen, but also a nationally televised display of police photographs depicting Brown Simpson as a bruised and battered wife. Next, in April 1995, Timothy McVeigh drove a truck of explosives into the Alfred P. Murrah Federal Building in downtown Oklahoma City, taking 168 lives and leaving over 800 injured. Nineteen of the victims were children in a day-care center. It was a violent time.

In 1995, the year we launched Week Without Violence, more than 2.5 million women were victims of violent crime, and nearly two-thirds knew or were related to their attackers. Violence against women took place—and still does—in big cities, seemingly idyllic suburbs, and rural areas alike. And most of it takes place in the home.

In order to be visible, valued, and heard, girls must also be safe, secure, and alive. The tragedy of Laquanda Edwards' death became a catalyst for positive action when Laquanda's mother, Lue Ella, founded the first Cabrini Green Girls Club in memory of her daughter. And the tragic circumstances of the nineties spurred the YWCA into action, too. The YWCA wanted to send the message that we can all take positive action against all forms of violence. The Week Without Violence addressed the entire range—violence on the streets, in schools, in the home, with guns, in gangs. Here is how the front page of the event organizer's kit explained the campaign:

Imagine

7 days

168 hours

10,080 minutes

604,080 seconds

WITHOUT VIOLENCE

Instead of using the event to complain about violence, we flipped the concept around and offered a vision of a community in peace. One of the ways we did this was by handing out informational cards to men on the street in Midtown Manhattan. The card was titled, "An Invitation to Men" and began:

> We know most of you would never beat your wife, your lover, or your child. We live and work with you. We love and respect you. You are our fathers, uncles, husbands, brothers, companions, friends, and lovers. But there are men who are violent:

The final line read:

> The next time you see or hear one of us in trouble, pay attention. We can't stop violence by ourselves. Join us.

I have handed out thousands of leaflets and brochures in my life for all sorts of causes. This is the only time I recall when not a single person who took a leaflet threw it away. Hundreds of men crossed the intersection of Fifty-third Street and Lexington Avenue carrying a reminder that it is up to each one of us to stop violence against women.

Did the YWCA Week Without Violence end violence against women? No. But I believe it made a contribution toward decreasing crime rates across the United States. And it demonstrated an important lesson: Complaining doesn't have to be loud or mean or angry to be effective. Instead it can be instructive and imaginative.

The Power of a Few Voices

While it takes guts to complain, it does not take a national organization or a significant budget to change your life or the world by acting on your complaints.

The Million Mom March

In August 1999, four years after the Week Without Violence, Donna Dees-Thomases, a New Jersey mother, read with horror about a gunman who randomly shot at a group of children in Granada Hills, California. Seven days later, on August 17, Donna decided to apply for a permit to march on Washington to protest this country's lack of meaningful gun laws.

Her individual protest grew into a grassroots movement of mothers called the Million Mom March (www.

millionmommarch.com). On May 14, 2000, approximately 750,000 mothers and others gathered on the National Mall in Washington, D.C., to demand sensible gun laws. An additional 150,000 to 200,000 people marched in support events across the country. Following the event, the Million Mom March participants became a chapter-based organization to promote sensible gun laws in state legislatures.

The Jersey Girls

The events of September 11, 2001, affected every American, but none more than the loved ones of people killed that day. One group of 9/11 widows from New Jersey banded together into a group they called the "Jersey Girls" and turned their personal grief into a powerful public complaint. The Jersey Girls stood out in the press and at public hearings pushing for a commission to determine what went wrong the day of the attacks and how to prevent it from happening again.

And they kept pushing. When Congress and the Bush administration stalled legislation, the Jersey Girls organized a rally with relatives of 9/11 victims on the steps of the Capitol, one of many trips they made to Washington. The women transformed themselves into sleuths and investigators, talking to the press and dogging lawmakers. Because of their relentless efforts, the National Commission on Terrorist Attacks finally was formed and held its first hearings in 2003. Is the commission perfect? Far from it. But no commission would exist at all were it not for the public complaints of these women.

Gaining from complaining is about turning one's frustrations, anger, or irritations into positive action. Like Donna Dees-Thomases and the Jersey Girls, you can achieve amazing things when you step out of line and stop waiting for someone else to fix the problems you see in your life or in the world. Like imagination, complaining, lobbying, and marching can be incredibly powerful.

How I Gained from Complaining

It's ironic that I'm championing complaining, because I personally have a low tolerance for complaining. This is probably because any sort of whining or complaining was deeply frowned upon in my family. My Irish grandmother and mother absolutely forbade it, often with the classic admonishment: "If you don't have anything nice to say, don't say anything at all." Even now, my eighty-three-year-old mother never complains. I don't know if that's a good thing or not, but it's a fact.

My father grew up in a working-class Italian family in New Jersey. He came from nothing and grew up to be a lawyer, leader, and politician. If we started complaining in front of my father, he would purse his lips and make a *zzt* sound that would shut us up immediately. My mother juggled the demands of five children, a manic-depressive mother, and an ambitious husband, and still served up a big meal each night, wearing perfume and heels. She managed all this on her own with no one to encourage or help her, and she never, ever complained.

Of course, there is a downside to having parents who do not tolerate complaining. I don't think I ever spoke to my parents about things that bothered or frightened me. This helped me to become confident and self-sufficient, but it also landed me in twenty years of therapy, where I finally had an opportunity to talk about my own complaints and understand my fears!

As you know, I experienced a difficult period in my mid-thirties, sparked by dissatisfaction with my career and life as a single woman in New York. I remember saying in my therapy sessions in those years that I felt like I was stuck in a tight parking space—every time I tried to move I would bang into the cars in front of and behind me. The pieces of my life didn't fit together anymore. Nothing excited or engaged me.

Perhaps you've had a similar stuck feeling in your life, or perhaps you feel that way now. The thing about feeling stuck is that it's also a secure feeling. It's familiar. Familiarity is a good thing in some situations. Are you stuck in something that is familiar and routine that is actually good and healthy? Or are you feeling stuck because you are dissatisfied and challenged? Stuck is not always bad. There can be value in staying stuck for a while. It's a time to think and feel and be. Honor feeling stuck.

Honor "Stuck"

Feeling stuck is not always a bad thing. When you acknowledge that you are feeling stuck, you can analyze the feeling: are you feeling stuck because you are set in a routine, or are you feeling stuck because you are unsatisfied with your life? Stuck provides an opportunity to be still for a while and figure out your next step.

As you learned in the last chapter, I was stuck for about three years. But after that period of imagining, searching, and exploring, I flourished. Today I am still enjoying the fruits of the life I began then, as a business owner and a happily married woman. If I hadn't given credence to the difficult feelings and acknowledged that I felt stuck, I don't think I would have been so successful afterward. By admitting my complaints about my life and working to change things I didn't like, I found my way to success and fulfillment.

Starting a Business from a Complaint

I am far from the only person to start a business from a feeling of dissatisfaction or not fitting in. In fact, feeling stuck, excluded, forgotten, or frustrated is the catalyst for a large number of start-ups. Here are some of the many women whose complaints have fueled their successful entrepreneurial ventures. Each woman is an example of how complaints can benefit one's own life (by providing the idea for a profitable business) and benefit other women (with jobs, plus new products and services).

Tamara Monosoff

Anybody who has ever had a toddler or puppy knows how they can wreak havoc with a roll of toilet paper. The puppies drag it all over the house and make a mess; the toddlers ball it up into huge wads and stop up the toilet. Parents and pet owners have been complaining about such things for years. Tamara Monosoff finally did something about it.

Tamara invented a product called the TP Saver. It's a gadget that prevents kids and pets from unraveling a toilet paper roll. Amazing right? And you might be more amazed when you learn about Tamara's background. Tamara holds a doctorate in education with a specialization in women and leadership. She held multiple positions at the White House and the U.S. Department of Education during the Clinton administration.

On the Web site www.MomInventors.com, Tamara tells her story of going from a presidential appointee to a toilet paper gadget inventor—and more:

> My husband and I had just moved back to Califor-
> nia, where I'd given birth to my first daughter. I had
> always loved working—especially my position as a
> presidential appointee to the Clinton administration
> at the White House and the U.S. Department of

Education. I wanted to continue using that part of my brain, but have more flexibility as a mom.

When my daughter grew into the toddler stage, she became intrigued with unraveling the toilet paper from the roll . . . I looked for a solution and didn't find it, so I decided to invent one myself. Voila—the TP Saver was born!

Instead of just complaining about her toddler's antics, Tamara created her own solution. If that wasn't enough, in the process, she realized that other women probably had similar ideas. So she decided to create a whole organization, called Mom Inventors (www.mominventors.com), to help other mom inventors take their products from concept to market. The company will also license and publicize mom inventions.

Tamara's fellow Mom Inventors provide more examples of private concerns made public. Each of the Mom Inventors has taken action and invented a product to do something about issues many women complain about. They make private issues public and assert their power to improve their lives—and the lives of other women.

Cristy Clarke

Have you ever felt completely bored at a cocktail party because everyone is making the same old small talk? Happens to the best of us, right? Mom inventor Cristy Clarke decided not to take the boredom anymore. She created a product, TableTopics (www.tabletopics.com), to liven up parties. TableTopics cards are printed with thought-provoking questions that are housed in a beautifully designed cube you can keep on a counter, coffee table, or dinner table.

Nina Restieri

Nina Restieri is a busy mom of four children, aged nine, seven, five, and two. Instead of just complaining about her crazy schedule, Nina created a product to make her life a little easier. She is a Make Mine a Million $ Business finalist and the inventor of momAgenda (www.mom agenda.com), the original day planner created for mothers. The planner's unique, week-at-a-view layout features separate spaces for mom and each child, allowing moms to manage multiple schedules. You may have seen Nina and her product on *The Today Show*. Thousands of moms have benefited from Nina's decision to stop waiting for the perfect product to come onto the market and create the exact planner a mom would need.

Leah Brown

Another Make Mine a Million $ Business awardee, Leah Brown, started a business from a very serious complaint—the length of time it takes to create new drugs. Her company, ATen (A10) Solutions (www.atensolutions.com), provides clinical trials for new drugs and specializes in getting results fast. Why did she start this company? Leah launched A10 because her uncle died of AIDS. She created the company to develop faster ways of bringing drugs to market, because it was too late for her uncle.

Liz Lange

After spending a year listening to all of her girlfriends complain that they couldn't find any good maternity clothes, she created Liz Lange Maternity (www.lizlange.com)—before she even had kids! The business, launched in 1997, became successful immediately, and Lange opened stores in New York and Beverly Hills. In 2002, she designed a more affordable maternity line for Target, to bring fashionable maternity clothes to women across the country. In 2006, Lange, now a mother of two, launched the "4th-trimester" line, to provide clothes for women who have just had babies and are not quite back to their pre-pregnancy shape. Based on her own experience and comments from her friends and customers, she knew that postpartum fashion would be a big hit.

Gaining from Complaining Can Lead to a Business Idea

Lest you think that women starting their own businesses are a "niche" group, please note that there are approximately 10.5 million women business owners today. Launching my business in 1988 was part of a larger trend of women's entrepreneurship taking place across the country. This trend stems from women getting the right to business credit in our own names in 1974, thanks to the Equal Credit Act, sponsored by

Congresswomen Bella Abzug and Lindy Boggs. Over the past thirty-plus years, a tidal wave of women have recognized that one of the ways to escape their complaints and frustration about rigid hours, glass ceilings, sexual harassment, or dissatisfaction with work or life was to create our own companies. The trend has only grown, of course. In 1974, about 5 percent of businesses were owned by women. Today, almost 50 percent are women-owned!

Women are running companies large and small in their basements, kitchens, garages, and spare rooms. Many of them developed innovative products and services at home while their children were at school or after they came home from their full-time jobs. Many of them left corporate jobs to have more flexibility. If you aren't familiar with the phenomenon of women running their own businesses, I hope you'll check out the Make Mine a Million $ Business Web site at www.makemineamillion.org.

Gaining from Complaining in Corporate America

If entrepreneurship is not for you, there are loads of other ways to change your career and find work that you love and that fulfills your financial needs. You are never stuck in a job. There are almost always options.

Nely Galán (www.nelygalan.com), emeritus board member of Count Me In, launched her company, Galan Entertainment, with the mandate of creating television content for the Latino market. Her company has successfully produced over six hundred episodes of programming in both

English and Spanish, bridging multiple television genres. Galan is the former president of entertainment for Telemundo, the Spanish-language powerhouse. In her book, *The Swan Curriculum,* Nely tells the story of overcoming her fears of asking for large sums of money by "channeling" a seventy-year-old Jewish man named Mel in her mind! Early in her career she worked for several older Jewish men, including TV pioneer Norman Lear. She loved the way he negotiated fearlessly, so she incorporated it into her approach.

When Telemundo was sold out from under her leadership, she decided to start her own production company. She received a call from Rupert Murdoch, who offered her a job. When they met to discuss the offer, Nely told Murdoch that she didn't want to work for him; she wanted to start her own business instead. As Nely tells the story, she channeled her imaginary alter ego Mel in the meeting and—knowing she needed $1 million to start her own company—asked Murdoch for five. He said yes.

Susan Sobbott, the mother of two young children, worked her way up at American Express and is now president of American Express OPEN, the small business network (www.open.americanexpress.com). To my great joy, she has used her leadership to accelerate the power of women entrepreneurs. Thanks to Susan, OPEN signed on as the Make Mine a Million $ Business program's founding sponsor. Susan convinced her company to help more women have the options of flexibility, success, and access to resources that she found at American Express. She is our champion inside American Express and has helped the company to understand how what's good for women is good for their bottom line.

EXERCISE: Gain from Your Complaints

It's okay to complain as long as you use your complaints as a catalyst for coming up with solutions. I recognized this early in my career as a union organizer. There were people who did nothing but complain about their jobs, yet they would not sign a union card. We would ask them for their ideas—"What would you do if you ran the unit?" The people who complained the most would rarely offer solutions. You need to act on your criticism! Don't just bring problems; focus on solutions!

That experience really stayed with me—this notion that if you don't like a situation, there are all kinds of ways to change it. Like Tamara Monosoff, Liz Lange, Nely Galán, Susan Sobbott, and so many other women, you can use challenges and complaints as catalysts. Instead of complaining for complaining's sake, take your anger, sadness, annoyance, frustration, or whatever you feel and turn it into a road map for creating a better product, business, and community. Ideas, direction, and passion can all come out of what is bugging you.

Start right now. Make a list of what drives you crazy, incenses you, makes your blood boil every time you see it or hear about it:

_____

_____

_____

_____

_____

_____

What draws you in or engages you every time you see it on the Internet, drive past it on the street, hear it on the radio, or read about it in a magazine?

_____

_____

_____

_____

Look at everything you've written above. What are the commonalities, the themes? What ideas can be combined to make a product, start a business, a nonprofit organization, a new initiative at work, a community service project, a hobby, a blog, a letter to the editor of your local newspaper? Write down the ways in which you can take action on something you've written above:

_____

_____

_____

_____

_____

_____

The Oldest Complaint in the World: Housework

It may not be at work that you feel stuck. Many women have gained from complaining in the private realm, at home. I'm talking about the frequent complaint that men don't do enough housework and child care. There are millions of places on the Web where you can find women complaining about unequal division of labor in the home, as well as more than a few rants from men complaining about women complaining about this topic. That's all just complaining for complaining's sake. Fortunately, many people are experimenting with progressive ways to solve the challenge of pursuing one's interests while living in a relatively clean home and eating square meals.

It can be hard to explore solutions to this challenge because the image of women as homemakers and men as breadwinners is so ingrained in our culture. But many families have found creative solutions to divide the labor at home so all members of a family can pursue their goals and interests. I used to do about half of the shopping for my household—my husband and me—and cooked two to three meals a week. Then, a few years ago, I broke my foot and could not do anything that required standing. Gary took over the shopping and cooking for a while. He discovered that he really liked doing it, and he has continued to do it. This may not work for everyone, but it works well for us. Being free of the cooking and shopping responsibilities has given me more time to devote to building Count Me In and the Make Mine a Million $ Business movement, and to writing this book. Gary seems to have recognized that and his shopping and cooking are his contribution to those goals.

That's just what works for us. Studies show that men do more housework than women think, but still not nearly half. According to a 2005 study of 265 married couples with children in the *Journal of Marriage and Family*, women shoulder an average of 61 percent of the housework, while men do an average of 39 percent. You might look at these numbers and compare them to your own life, or you may be a single woman without anyone to share the burden. But what is more important is to decide what balance works for your unique situation. Instead of complaining about an unfair burden, figure out a solution that will make your life more enjoyable. All that matters is that the solution works for you.

There are also many new products and services that can help ease women's complaints about housework. One example is Internet grocery delivery services, such as Peapod and FreshDirect. In a survey of women participating in the Make Mine a Million $ Business program, I was struck by the number of women who cited grocery delivery as one of the key factors in their success! Who would have thought that eliminating regular trips to the local supermarket could be so powerful?

Women inventors are working on ways to eliminate complaints about housework as well. For instance, Helen Grunier, an engineer-turned-robotics-entrepreneur, received venture capital funding with help from Springboard Enterprises (www.springboardenterprises.org—a nonprofit organization that accelerates women's access to the equity markets) to create the Roomba, the saucer-shaped, ankle-high machine that circles the floor, bounces off walls, and slips easily under furniture to do your vacuuming for you. Technology can set you free from much of the housework—and the complaining about the housework—that has kept women tied to the home. Again, a woman business owner has created a product out of a common complaint.

To Change Your Life, Change the Things You Complain About—Even Laundry

If your vision of your ideal life does not include hours of housework, then you need to clearly plan how things will get done. Don't wait or wish or hope that a solution will magically appear. Think about the housework you complain about and decide what you and your family can do to get everything done. You might create a rotating schedule of chores that includes everyone in your family. Perhaps, if you can afford it, you hire a cleaning person so you don't have to do everything yourself. Or, maybe you can lower your standards a bit and decide that a perfectly clean house is not so important after all.

Gaining from Complaining About Child Care: EquallySharedParenting.com

In the 1975 book *The Mermaid and the Minotaur,* Dorothy Dinnerstein asserts that until men and women equally share the task of raising children, cultural equality will never happen. I agree that our parents have a tremendous impact on our lives and shape our beliefs about male and female roles. If men and women are to share power equally in the public sphere, we must also share power and responsibility equally in the private sphere of the home.

EquallySharedParenting.com is a Web site dedicated to women and men who want to share equally in the raising of their children, household chores, breadwinning, and recreation. This site is the brainchild of Marc and Amy Vachon, consultants in equal parenting and equal parents themselves. "Half the work; all the fun" is their positive empowering tagline. The Web site offers a blog, step-by-step guides, resource lists, real-life stories, and more. Marc and Amy's introduction to the concept of equally shared parenting even begins with my favorite word:

> Imagine a life without having to choose between a meaningful career and enough time with your children. Envision that while you are at work, your wonderful children are safe, happy, healthy, and growing in the care of someone who loves them just as much as you do. At home, you spend many hours with them each week to connect with and nurture them. There is plenty of time for yourself and your favorite hobbies as well, and you never have to do more than half of the housework. The burden of earning the family's income no longer falls on just one of you. You are fully competent as a parent rather than an understudy or

manager to your spouse, and you have an energized marriage with a fun and happy partner.

The Vachons, who were featured in a June 2008 *New York Times Magazine* cover story by Lisa Belkin, are gaining from a decades-old complaint. Not only are they offering their own solutions, but they also invite others who are trying to equally share household duties to join their online community and share their advice and stories. This model is not right for everyone, but it is a positive, solution-oriented model that is available to anyone with access to a computer and an Internet connection.

Complaining About Ourselves

The energy women spend complaining about housework, men, or children is undoubtedly dwarfed by the energy we spend criticizing ourselves. How can we use complaints about ourselves—our looks, our weight, our intelligence, our abilities—as a catalyst to live the lives we want, rather than let it be a force that leaches our power?

I'll never forget when I first read Susie Orbach's *Fat Is a Feminist Issue* in 1978. As I was reading the book, I made and ate two ham sandwiches slathered in mayonnaise! It was one of the first times in my adult life that I didn't feel bad about eating.

My biggest takeaway from the book was to listen to your body—it tells you what and when it needs food, rest, and exercise. Eat when you're hungry and stop when you're full.

Orbach, who was the eating disorder specialist who helped Princess Diana, recommended an exercise she called the "supermarket fantasy." The directions were to go to the supermarket and buy absolutely everything that you want. The trick is to buy more, not less. The first time I did the exercise, I remember buying several cakes and quarts and quarts of ice cream—the foods that I had been admonished not to eat since I was nine years old.

The exercise was scarily exciting. I was literally looking over my shoulder at the supermarket, worrying about what people were thinking. But I did it. And sure enough my clothes started to fit me better. According to Orbach, it is the forbiddenness of these foods that makes them so attractive. Abundance, not scarcity, is what made it possible for me to be healthy and fit.

Another life-changing recommendation in *Fat Is a Feminist Issue* was to get rid of any clothes that were the least bit uncomfortable or tight. The whole time you are sitting in tight clothes, you are being reminded of what you don't like about your body. To this day, I don't wear clothes that are tight or confining.

When we wear clothes that don't fit, women feel like we don't fit. Like we don't belong.

There is nothing wrong with wanting to lose weight if you are unhappy with your size. The problem is with the notion that our value is determined by our body parts or shape or size. Remember back to the goal of Take Our Daughters to Work Day: for girls and women to be visible, valued, and heard. We are all valuable, no matter what our size. It is most important that we value ourselves.

EXERCISE: What in Your Life Doesn't "Fit"?

What are the things in your life that don't "fit"? Identifying aspects of your life that feel "tight" is a great first step to shedding them. Perhaps you feel stifled by the rules of your workplace or church. Or maybe you are tired of the amount of time you spend picking up after your children when they could be helping you. Or maybe the competitiveness of the women in your book group just doesn't fit you anymore. Or the boyfriend or husband who puts you down. Or the cigarettes in your purse and that persistent cough. Maybe watching so much television doesn't fit the life you really want to lead. Take some time here to think about what feels tight or constraining and doesn't fit you or your life anymore, and write those things down here:

What *Fat Is a Feminist Issue* and its lessons changed for me is the belief that I have to fit someone else's definition of who I should be and how I should look. Ever since childhood I tried to fit into someone else's clothes—beginning with a Catholic school uniform with a white bib and green-and-white plaid pleated skirt. By finally accepting my body—which took years of therapy in addition to reading a book—I developed a much deeper understanding of who I was and what I really wanted to do. I stopped complaining about my body around the same time I stopped complaining about my career and started my own business.

There is so much more in the world to do and enjoy—why waste your power and time thinking too much about your looks? I loved an article I read in *O Magazine*, in which a woman describes running into an old boyfriend and chatting with him about the old days. She tells him she remembers always worrying while they were having sex that her thighs were too fat. "Oh, yes," he says with a grin. "All these years I've been wanting to talk to you about your thighs." She says it was only at that moment that she realized how silly her worry was.

Here is a shocking fact. According to a survey by *Fitness* magazine, 21 percent of women would give up ten years of their lives to achieve their ideal weight. Eighty-five percent of women surveyed would rather have an extra toe than an extra fifty pounds! It is a complete myth that once you lose weight, your life will be perfect. Work on your life first.

Your Body Really Is a Temple

Like the nuns told me in second grade, your body is a temple.

If you want to stop waiting for good things to happen in your life, stop "weighting." Your body listens to all the bad things you say about

> it. Complaining about your body drains your energy and your time and
> your joy.

Eight Weeks to Doing Less of What You Complain About, More of What You Want

You are never completely stuck, because there are almost always options. Even if you feel completely paralyzed, you can start with tiny steps to move yourself out of your stuckness. My belief in this baby-step approach comes from one of my favorite books, *Eight Weeks to Optimum Health*, by Dr. Andrew Weil. His message is that you can slowly become healthier if you start doing positive things. Every day, just do a little bit more of what you really want to do, such as walking, eating vegetables, or drinking water. This approach is about filling time with what we want to do, versus what we mindlessly do—TV, shopping, kids, spouse, grooming.

A friend of mine is an excellent example of how baby steps can add an enormous amount to your life. She shared with me the fact that she had loved singing in high school, but in college had auditioned for an exclusive a capella singing group and was rejected. After that, she lost her confidence and completely stopped singing—for ten years. Over time, she admitted to herself that she really missed it. She felt way too intimidated to join a chorus, so as a first step she went to iTunes and downloaded all of her favorite Broadway show tunes to her iPod. After listening to them for a while, she started quietly singing along.

A few months later, she went online, to Google, and typed in "Broadway singing + New York City + no auditions necessary" and, to her surprise, she found a weekly open singing group just a few subway stops from her apartment. Feeling too shy to go to the group, she called the teacher and got a referral for private lessons. "Something happened when I started singing again, even though it was just a few lessons," she told me. "I honestly feel so much more joyful."

She had, quite literally, found her voice. There is infinite benefit to taking even one hour out of your week to sing or do anything that gives you pure joy. Your baby steps can involve spending a few minutes a day in meditation, karate, gardening, reading poetry, or anything at all. Just start doing it.

Still not feeling ready to move forward in a new direction, even in baby steps? Take a browse through Netflix or your local video store. Why do you think movies like *The Shawshank Redemption, Spartacus, Gladiator, Working Girl, 9-to-5, The Queen,* and *Pretty Woman* are so incredibly popular? People love stories of heroes who are seemingly stuck in impossible situations—prison, slavery, prostitution, the depths of public opinion—who use their ingenuity and personal strength to escape, rise above it, and turn things around. At some basic level, we all want to believe that we can change our lives. Inspiration is a powerful antidote to complaining.

EXERCISE: Who Are Your Heroes?

Take a moment to think of your favorite heroes of fiction or movies or real life. Go back to your answers to the Proust Questionnaire and add a few more names. List your favorite heroes and why you admire them. Your answers may offer a hint to something you want in your life.

Gaining from Complaining in Public: Anita Hill and Anucha Browne Sanders

Anita Hill and Anucha Browne Sanders are two of the women on my hero list. Their stories provide two of the most public and profound examples of gaining from complaining.

Mention of Anita Hill's 1991 congressional testimony continues to elicit extreme passion—both positive and negative—more than seventeen years after the fact. Professor Hill courageously testified about Clarence Thomas's sexual harassment on national television. In front of the whole country, Hill took her complaint to Congress and moved sexual harassment from a hidden private world into the public arena.

Hill spoke out because Thomas's advances and comments were unwelcome, unwanted, and illegal. Her testimony raised serious questions about his character and possible conduct as a Supreme Court Justice. I watched some of the hearings with my best friend Beth Korein at her grandmother's apartment. Beth's grandma Sarah was muttering at the TV that "the girl should have kept her mouth shut." Sarah was a very accomplished woman; they called her the Bella Abzug of real estate. She had amassed power and wealth, but she still believed that women should keep quiet about sexual harassment. Beth and I, however, cheered each time Hill responded strongly to a nasty or stupid question from one of the senators.

Some might have argued that Hill—and women in general—did not gain from her testimony. Immediately following the hearings, public opinion polls showed that 47 percent of those polled believed Thomas, while only 24 percent believed Hill. I take a longer-term view. By 1992, public opinion polls showed 44 percent believed Hill and only 34 percent believed Thomas. The tide turned slowly, but dramatically. This case made sexual harassment a household phrase.

I remember a meeting I attended on Capitol Hill in 1989, when I was networking to get clients for my new business. It was the aftermath of a presidential campaign year, when I had worked on the Dukakis campaign, and it was a meeting of seasoned women campaign workers. We were networking about new jobs and talking in general about what people's experiences had been. While we were chatting, some of the women tried to steer younger women away from jobs with lecherous U.S. representatives. Astonishingly, though, the seasoned women would not name names. It was ridiculous!

I asked why they didn't simply name the names of the offenders so that no woman would go work for them—or at least would not be surprised when her boss tried to stick his tongue down her throat. My suggestion of outing the elected congressional sexual harassers was voted down by women who worked on the Hill, because they were afraid of losing their jobs.

These women thought that they were stuck—stuck working for lascivious men, stuck in secrecy. It is natural to feel this way when you are afraid. But they weren't stuck. They could have taken action and eventually, years later, they did.

After Anita Hill's testimony as well as the breaking of the 1991 Tailhook Scandal, in which female naval officers were sexually abused by pilots at a Las Vegas convention, things changed. In 1992, eight congressional staffers made statements to the *Seattle Times* alleging that Senator Brock Adams (D-Wash.) had committed various acts of sexual misconduct, ranging from sexual harassment to rape. The women, who had been afraid of losing their jobs just a few years earlier, brought down a United States senator. Poetically, he was replaced by Senator Patty Murray, a suburban mom.

In the end, Anita Hill's accusations heightened public

awareness of sexual harassment in the workplace and women's unequal representation in the political sphere. Her testimony also contributed to what became known as the "Year of the Woman," the 1992 presidential election year, when a significant number of women were simultaneously elected to the federal legislative branch, Janet Reno became the first female U.S. attorney general, and Hillary Clinton the first first lady who had financially supported her family. All of these developments helped lead to passage of the Violence Against Women Act in 1994, which provided $1.6 billion to enhance investigation and prosecution of violent crimes against women. The National Organization for Women (www.now.org) called the bill "the greatest breakthrough in civil rights for women in nearly two decades."

Personally, Anita Hill's testimony had a massive impact on my view of the world. There would be no Take Our Daughters to Work Day without Anita Hill. Her testimony helped me see the workplace as the location to transform girls' lives and how they were viewed by others.

Fifteen years later, in November 2007, another prominent man faced allegations of sexual harassment by an employee. This time, she won. After Anucha Browne Sanders was fired from a high-ranking executive position for the New York Knicks, she filed a sexual harassment lawsuit against the Knicks' general manager Isiah Thomas and Madison Square Garden, the corporation that owns the Knicks and several other New York sports franchises. The suit claimed that Thomas sexually harassed her and then fired her in retaliation for her complaints about the alleged harassment. A jury believed her testimony and she received an $11.6 million judgment.

It is far from easy to file a sexual harassment lawsuit, especially against a former star basketball player and prominent public figure. To make the decision, Browne Sanders sought the advice of Billie Jean King, herself a woman who went public with her complaints about the lack of fair treatment of women in the world of tennis. According to a report in *The New York Times* (November 1, 2007), King advised Browne Sanders to "just do whatever is your truth."

Ultimately, Browne explained why she decided to pursue her public complaint against Thomas and Madison Square Garden. The *Times* article read:

> Browne Sanders said she thought of her deceased mother, Alma, who refused to swim during physical education class because the pool was open to African Americans during only the final period of the school week, right before a regular cleaning. She also thought of her 13-year-old daughter, who will one day enter the workforce.
>
> "You can't compromise yourself," Browne Sanders said. "I hope we're teaching young women that we're past the days where we had to put up with a bad work environment."

Browne Sanders is right. Her actions, like those of Anita Hill, will have positive ramifications for years. That is the essence of gaining from complaining. Browne Sanders's court victory seems to me to be a sign that women's power is changing. People believed her when she spoke out. Women's voices of complaint have power.

Being inspired, talking about solutions, and taking action are the ultimate antidotes to complaining. When you are busy, you don't have time to complain. When you are moving forward and making a difference, you lose the desire to focus on your problems. When you air your complaints in a positive, proactive, public way, you can address them and find other people who can support you. You can find the tools and resources to deal with life's big and small challenges. And challenges are the focus of the next chapter: overcoming the setbacks that may crop up as you step out of line and pursue your own path.

WHAT IS HOLDING YOU BACK?

For years after Take Our Daughters to Work Day, I was introduced at speaking engagements as the woman to call if you want to think big. I am always a little flattered, challenged, and intimidated by those remarks. I loved the recognition for my contribution and I continued to think big. But it can be hard to top a success like that and to feel as though any event with less than 71 million participants will fall short!

In April 2000, I experienced an event that not only "fell short" of my and other people's expectations, I think it's fair to say that it pretty much bombed. However, this overwhelming setback set the stage for a new direction in my career. What I learned is that failure, fear, and frustration—all of which are part of my story—are pretty much inevitable when you choose to step out of line. What matters is how you handle the setbacks.

This story begins at the Museum for Television and Radio, where I was part of a team launching a new nonprofit organization called Count Me In for Women's Economic Independence. Women leaders from TV, the Internet, finance, and media were there. They all pledged to reach out to their constituents, members, viewers, and friends a month later asking them to contribute $5 or more over the Internet to create a multimillion dollar loan fund to help women start businesses. The idea was that women would help women, and all using the Web.

My greatest moment of professional self-doubt and second-guessing came a few days after we launched Count Me In to the public. We had been on the front page of the *Wall Street Journal,* and iVillage.com had sent out over 12 million e-newsletters about the new organization. The Oxygen network (www.oxygen.com) had promoted us on cable TV, Working Woman Network promoted us online, and virtually every woman's organization sent an e-mail to its members on our behalf. Talk about not knowing where to be on the day of an event—everything in this case took place over the Internet. All we could do was wait for people to visit the Web site, open e-mails, and make a contribution, and hopefully watch the loan money start pouring in.

We were counting on raising $25 to $50 million for our fund in a few days—that was what all the "experts" told us—to help thousands of women start micro businesses, get education, and borrow money in an emergency. We figured if every woman in America sent in $5 over the Internet or through the mail, then we could help women zoom into their full potential in the U.S. economy and step into their power.

Wow, were we wrong.

Women at that time were not comfortable sending money over the Internet. The dot-com boom was beginning to crumble. Count Me In didn't have any track record of making loans to women. No one had made micro-loans over the Internet. We had spent most of the money we had raised to launch our Web site and our campaign to raise millions, and now we were stuck with no funds to make loans. We didn't know it at the time, but the dot-com crash was about to happen and make the situation even worse.

I felt physically ill for the first couple of days—almost unable to breathe—disappointed and ashamed that Count Me In had not "worked" the way we had planned. We raised about $150,000, which was a far cry from $25 to $50 million. I would wake up with that feeling that you have when someone you love is very sick or near death—you wake up refreshed and then suddenly remember your dying loved one and feel so sad and lost. I stayed home in this numb state with my husband the first weekend after we launched the campaign, feeling like a failure. How could I have imagined something so clearly, something that women had responded to so well in the planning stages, and not succeed?

Still, I kept moving forward, talking to people and sharing my vision. It wasn't easy, but I kept pursuing the vision. Eventually, American Express loaned us some money to make micro-loans so that we could prove our concept. On August 9, 2000, we made our first loan to Amy's Bread (www.amysbread.com), a bakery owned by a woman in New York City.

It was a wonderful moment, but the program still didn't take off. One day, I winced to read that, according to the U.S. Census, women owned nearly half of the nation's privately held businesses, but four times as many men as women owned companies that earned more than $1 million a year. Specifically, there were nearly 10.5 million women-owned businesses, but only 243,000 were at the million dollar revenue mark. I wondered if this was part of our problem. In fact, these statistics coincided with a troublesome trend I'd noted in our programs at Count Me In, where some of the loan recipient businesses had begun to plateau at $250,000 in revenue. Women who had been so excited about getting their businesses off the ground found themselves hesitant or incapable of taking the next step, to expand past micro-business and self-employment into larger enterprises that would create jobs and build wealth not just for themselves, but their families and communities. While some women were simply happy being their own bosses and genuinely wanted to keep their businesses small, many others were staying small because they didn't know how to get bigger and needed help doing it.

As we analyzed the data and talked to more and more women, the specific problems with Count Me In became clear: we had focused on what women lack, which is access to credit and capital, and we'd focused on starting very small businesses, which we learned women could figure out how to do without us. Once we focused on what women could do, which was start and build businesses, and that what they needed was help navigating the growth, we finally found the right formula. By focusing on helping women grow the businesses they already had, Count Me In took off and we launched our signature program, Make Mine a Million $ Business, which has become an unqualified success.

Quite simply, if Count Me In had not struggled or if I had given up after the initial failure, Make Mine a Million $ Business may not have been born. Setbacks can be the greatest catalysts for success if you acknowledge their lessons and keep moving forward to achieve your goals.

The Three Cs

As we began to focus on helping women's businesses grow, we found that, despite the great strides women entrepreneurs were making, they were in need of three crucial elements: 1) greater confidence, 2) capital, and 3) a community of women trying to do the same things. To achieve their business goals, women need access to a diverse menu of resources that includes confidence-building, coaching, technology, markets, community, and capital.

Guess what? These are the things that hold women back from achieving anything we want in our lives, not just growing businesses. These three things—the three Cs—can slow down your momentum as you are trying to make changes. They can make you stop believing or never even get started. And—good news—there are many tools you can use to overcome these potential obstacles in your path.

The *C* Words Cheat Sheet

To achieve your goals embrace these essential elements:

- Confidence: Comes from inside you. Get clear on what you are good at, where you are competent, and confidence will flow from there. Don't look to others for confidence—no one can give it to you. Believe in yourself and that you can have it your way.

- Capital: Knowing that you "need money" is not enough. Make a detailed plan and be very specific about exactly how you will use it. Be clear about how you will pay it back.

- Community: Find a group of like-minded people and get involved. No one achieves anything alone. There is a world of help, support, and camaraderie available to you on whatever life path you choose.

In this chapter, we'll dig deeper into the first two Cs: confidence and capital. In chapter 6, we'll explore the importance of community.

Get Your Confidence Level Up to Your Skill Level

My friend Lane Wallace is a flight instructor and a pilot. The vast majority of pilots (90 percent) are men so Lane teaches a lot of men. She told me that from her observations, the key difference between male pilots and female pilots is the gap between the skill level and confidence levels of each group. The challenge with men, Lane said, is to bring their skill level up to their confidence level. With women, it's the exact opposite. The challenge for women, she says, is to bring their confidence level up to their skill level. Think about that for a minute. There are thousands of confident men flying around who need better skills and women with good skills who lack the confidence to really fly.

Sound familiar? Many women can relate to this. So many women who are experienced, well-educated, talented, and more tell me that they struggle with the feeling of not being enough, not knowing enough to go to the next level.

It's time for a reality check. The simple fact is that if you have successfully completed projects at work, planned a wedding, raised children, applied to and been accepted to college, served in the military, started a business, bought a home, figured out how to post an item on eBay, found a job, or competed in sports, then you can figure out most anything. This is where we need to take a page from the men's book—confidence leads the way to competence.

Exercise: What Are You Good At?

First write down twenty things that you are good at.

I'm good at the following things—you can write your list next to mine:

Bike riding

Swimming

Inspiring people

Mobilizing large numbers of people

Baking cakes

Prioritizing

Telling stories

Talking to the press

Raising Money

Attracting the right kind of attention

Going to the gym

Listening

Being a friend

Being a daughter

Being a sister

Being a wife

Being a stepmother

Being an auntie

Roasting a chicken

The vision thing

Now, drawing on the list, what five things emerge as your areas of strength? These are the things I am best at:

1. *Marriage, family, and friends*
2. *Vision and strategic thinking*

3. *Inspiring and mobilizing others*
4. *Storytelling, speeches, and interviews*
5. *Staying healthy and physically active*

Now do yours.

1.
2.
3.
4.
5.

Memorize what you are best at. Keep the list with you so you can tap into your confidence whenever you need it.

I see the power of confidence in practice at every Make Mine a Million $ Business event across the country. The most inspiring moments for me are the rehearsals and public presentations, when each woman business owner stands up in front of a large audience, introduces herself and her business and explains why her business can reach $1 million or more in revenues and how she will do it.

The women stand with shaking hands and trembling voices and tell about their visions for the future—about their software development firms, construction businesses, spa services, consulting firms, catering enterprises, retail stores, vineyards, and more.

Some begin speaking with their hair in their eyes and their heads hung low like they are giving a book report in the sixth grade, but with some tough love and coaching they grow more confident as they realize that something special is happening, something that many of them had not experienced much before: They are being listened to. And taken seriously. They have stepped out of line to say, "Stop, look, and listen to me! I have a business, I want to grow my business bigger and faster, and I need help."

One of those women was Charlene Foster of Baraboo, Wisconsin. Charlene is the mother of five children, whom she homeschools. She is also the owner of an organic diaper business called Tiny Tush (www.tinytush.com). Charlene was a finalist in the Make Mine a Million $ Business program a few years ago, and she struggled in the practice sessions before her big moment in front of the judging panel. She was very nervous and couldn't seem to articulate the success of her business and what she needed to grow it. She had brought her husband and all five children, including her adolescent daughter, along for support.

After a particularly frustrating attempt to present, she walked off the stage and told one of our staff members, Libby, that she was quitting. She said she just couldn't make the presentation.

Libby replied, "What are you going to tell your children if you quit?"

That one question gave Charlene the determination she needed. Knowing that she was raising five children reminded her of how capable she was. Knowing that she wanted her children to be confident reminded her that she was a role model for them. She was still nervous, but she gathered enough confidence to change her mind and give her presentation. It wasn't the best presentation in the world, but it was honest and she had great answers to the questions about her business. Guess what? She won an award package and is now well on her way to $1 million in annual revenue.

This happens over and over again at Make Mine a Million $ Business events. Women step into their confidence and whole new worlds of possibility and opportunity open up. This can happen for you, too.

Tool for Gaining Confidence: Ban the S Word

If you struggle with confidence issues, there are tools you can use to increase your confidence and keep it strong in the face of inevitable challenges. One way to build your confidence muscle is to eliminate the nasty S word from your vocabulary: *should.* That word creeps into our thoughts and statements about money, power, marriage, kids, body size, career, lifestyle—whatever it is that you've been taught to equate with success or happiness. The "shoulds" have become an epidemic in women's lives and we've got to stop it. Having confidence in yourself means not blindly accepting what other people tell you should make you happy.

What sorts of "shoulds" might you want to eliminate from your consciousness? Here are just a few that women have shared with me, and how I would suggest rephrasing them. After reading through this list, take a stab at rewriting your own "shoulds."

The "Should"	The Rephrase
"All women should have children."	"I make a decision about having children that is right for me."
"One should never talk about money."	"I talk about money with people who support my financial goals."
"I should use my law degree to make a lot of money."	"I use my law degree to do work that I love."
"I should weigh less than my husband."	"I weigh a healthy and normal weight for me."
"Marriage should last forever."	"It can be healthy to exit an abusive marriage."

Now add your "shoulds" and your rephrases. Be sure to state them in the present tense to show that you are actively living this reality now and not in the future!

My "Shoulds"	My "Rephrases"

Tool for Gaining Confidence: Be Grateful for Challenges and Criticism

In chapter 1 we talked about the importance of resisting resistance. Well, the tricky thing about resistance is that it rears its sneaky little head more than once when you're in the process of changing your life. And resistance can be a real confidence killer. It comes in many forms, even from your family and people you consider to be close friends or colleagues. Women who take control of their love lives and put up online dating profiles are warned by friends that they might be stalked by crazy men. Women who start their own businesses are reminded by their lawyers and accountants of the failure rate of entrepreneurial enterprises. Children can be critical and even frightened as their mothers try a new way to live. Women who write books are reminded by their agents about harsh critics. Your husband, partner, or parents want to protect you because they doubt your ability or do not share your vision. Women who run for office are told by advisors that they'll have to become cold and cutthroat.

No matter what forms of resistance you face, here is a trick for overcoming resistance over and over again. It's not always an easy thing to do, but it works: Keep reminding yourself that you always have a choice in the way you respond. You can listen to resistance or criticism and let it hold you back, or you can listen to what people say in their criticism, understand why they might be saying it, and then decide whether the critique makes your idea, product, or decision stronger. If so, incorporate it.

If not, move on. You can use criticism as helpful information about another point of view. You can be confident in your own idea while understanding that failure is always a possibility. You can treat setbacks as information rather than an emotional knockout. You can take the positive position that challenges, pitfalls and resistance tell us things—these are the opportunities to learn the most!

Use Resistance

Resistance is common when you try to do almost anything, particularly things that are original and creative. And it often becomes more pronounced the better the idea you have. So keep your eyes and heart open. People will tell you what they are afraid of and you can address it or ignore it. Just don't be cowed by it.

When Sara Blakely, founder of the incredibly successful Spanx hosiery and clothing company (www.spanx.com), started to tell people about her idea to create footless pantyhose, she received nothing but discouragement. Several patent lawyers she approached thought her idea was so crazy that they asked if she'd been sent to them by a *Candid Camera*–type reality TV show. Manufacturers told her the idea of footless pantyhose made no sense and would never sell. But Sara knew she had a good idea and ignored all the naysayers. Just seven years later, she has turned her original $5,000 investment in the idea into more than $150 million in retail sales, four patents, a new brand at Target, and hundreds of media appearances. Now she is also helping other women build their confidence and access to opportunities through the Sara Blakely Foundation (www.sarablakelyfoundation.com), which provides education and entrepreneurial support for women around the globe.

Show Me the Money

In the last chapter we talked about determining your values. You also need to determine your value. And yes, I mean your monetary value. You can do this whether you own a business, work for someone else, work at home taking care of a household, or contribute any other form of work. There are ways to attach monetary value to the work that you do, so that you can place some number on it if that is helpful to you. Part of determining your value—whether you literally assign a number to your worth or not—is about busting that illusion that someone else will take care of you. The reason I founded Count Me In is because I know that women need our own money in order to live the lives we want.

If this notion makes you uncomfortable, then this concept is even more important for you to accept. There is a long-standing taboo around women and money that we need to break through once and for all. Of all the arenas where women most need to step out of line, stretch our imaginations, extend our reach, and hone our ambitions, none is more essential than the realm of money and power. Financial self-sufficiency—managing, saving, and investing our own money—says that women know our true value and have real power in the world.

One reason women avoid focusing on making and managing money is that once you put these facts down on paper, there are no illusions or gauzy fantasies. There is nothing to hide behind, no secret box to be opened, no hidden staircase that offers retreat. Either you have the money or you don't. The facts tell a story that cannot be banished with magical thinking.

Here are the big picture facts: Caucasian women currently earn 76 cents to a man's dollar; black women earn about 60 cents and Latinas about 55 cents. Two-thirds of all employed women in the U.S. earn $30,000 per year or less, according to the Older Women's League. The median full-time female income in 2004 was $31,223 as compared to $40,798 for men. Up until 1970, women in some states who wanted to control their own property had to petition the state for legal recognition that they could do so. And women weren't permitted to hold credit in their own names in many states until 1974. In the scheme of things, these prohibitions are recent realities, and their effects still influence our expectations and the attitude of the culture around us.

I am not alone in the belief that women need to overcome money fears, determine our value, and take control of our finances. Oprah Winfrey (www.oprah.com) and financial guru Suze Orman recently teamed up on the "Save Yourself" campaign for women (www.suzeorman. com), based on Orman's book, *Women and Money,* so all women could have access to financial knowledge. Suze's tagline is very clear: "Take control of your life by taking control of your finances." Having your own money means being for yourself. You can't be much clearer than using the title "Save Yourself," can you?

My Experience with Money Fears

It may surprise you to learn that I have faced serious doubts about my financial self-sufficiency. Despite my rebel core, I've dragged around my own complex and contradictory attitudes about money. I'll share two stories about how "capital" has held me back in my life, both at work and at home.

The first story relates to starting my own business. Until that point, I felt more comfortable focusing on other people's money, and told myself that I couldn't have mine until everyone else had theirs. I felt a certain squeamishness about wealth in general, along with a surprising envy whenever I considered another woman who was more financially successful than I was. There seemed to be a shame attached to having money and a shame attached to not having it—no wonder I was frustrated! It was sobering to realize that I, the independent, single woman who had always supported herself, still harbored an inner good girl, sitting on the side in her party frills, a girl who didn't want to be considered greedy, who still heard her mother's voice whispering that the whole topic of money was rude.

I eventually found my financial way by getting rid of the "should" that it was rude to talk about money. When I got serious about starting my own business, I started asking other entrepreneurs how to attach a price tag to my time and my work. As often happens, once you decide to reach out and seek help, the answer is relatively easy to find.

I received my answer from Norman Levy, a consultant I had known since 1980. I met Norman in a restaurant because he was doing this very loud imitation of Ed Koch. It was a fabulous impression and my friend Beth and I were falling down laughing. He finally came over to the table and mentioned he was a fan of my father. Years later, Norman was the person I took to lunch (no Ed Koch impression this time!) to ask for advice. I just came right out and said, "How do you know how much money to ask for from a client?"

Like many businessmen, Norman was completely comfortable talking about money and had no problem answering my question. He said, "Write down your exact monthly expenses—what you need to live. Remember that what you live on when you get a paycheck is what you make, not what you need or what you are worth. First write down only what you need—rent, food, therapy, whatever—and then go get a contract or two to cover those expenses."

My terror about starting my consulting practice was gone. I couldn't believe it was that simple. I remember my conversation with Norman being one of the most liberating conversations I'd ever had. And I followed his exact advice. I wrote down my monthly expenses. After that, I quickly got two contracts that covered my expenses and more. Any contracts above that were pure gravy. The simplicity of it all was amazing to me. Once I got over my "should" and asked for help, money was no different or more mystical than any other area of my life. The first year I was in business I made over $100,000!

EXERCISE: Determine How Much Money You Need

To determine how much money you need to make, follow the same instructions that Norman Levy gave me. Write down what you *need*: all of your basic expenses, the amount of money it takes to cover your necessities. Now write down how much money you *want* to have your life exactly your way. It's not magic.

My second story about money comes from my personal life. Sometimes a setback will come from a place you least expect it, and that was the case for me. I thought that starting my own business, supporting myself before and after marriage, and launching Count Me In had helped me conquer my money issues. I was wrong. In 2002, when

my husband quit his high-paying job, I found myself be-
having like a woman I didn't recognize. Gary had been unhappy with his job for a long time, but after 9/11, his
discontent grew stronger.

I had been urging him for years to be true to himself, to
find another position or create a business of his own. But
when he did just that—started his own business working
from home—I was unnerved and upset. Was I expected to
shoulder more of the financial burden in our partnership?
Would I be the main wage earner in our household? How
dare he actually make less than I did!

Of course, this reaction didn't make any sense. We had
always had separate finances and Gary's money was never
a factor in our marriage. I'd married him because he was
calm, funny, and smart, and I knew I'd enjoy my life far
more with him as my partner. But some other version of
me was furious and indignant, even contemplating divorce.
Eventually I returned to therapy with a sad tale of woe I'd
concocted, acting as if my life were over because my husband had liberated himself from a soul-deadening job.

My therapist set me straight. "If you're so worried about
money, go out and find new contracts yourself. You've always been able to earn money. Stop putting this unrealis-
tic level of pressure on your husband."

She was right. What old Doris Day film had I suddenly
fallen into? How had I ended up in *Pillow Talk* or *A Touch
of Mink,* where Doris dabbles in a career while flirting her
way to what she really wants—a fine catch in the form of
a caretaking husband? This was a sobering experience, a

reminder of how strongly these traditional views of women's and men's roles can grip us all. Happily, Gary now has a successful home-based business and has become a magical realist painter, capturing the fabled water towers that populate the New York City skyline (www.theviewoutmy window.com). And his paintings are selling.

The message here is that your financial security is your responsibility. You may decide that you will share that responsibility with a significant other, but it is a total myth that someone else will take care of your financial well-being. Unfortunately, many women learn this lesson too late, when they are facing a divorce.

Overcoming a Financial Setback: Dawn's Divorce

While my marriage survived, around this same time I watched in alarm as my friend Dawn's long partnership dissolved. With almost half of marriages ending in divorce, this situation is all too common. Dawn was the quintessential twenty-first-century woman, juggling a long marriage with her lawyer husband, two children, a career in a fragile nonprofit, an apartment in New York, and a vacation home in the Hamptons. A great cook and entertainer, Dawn catered to her husband, children, and guests with southern charm. I rarely saw her sit still—she was always cooking, talking, organizing, and socializing. She had one of those prosperous and creative lives you read about in women's magazines, and wonder, blearily, how she could possibly manage it all.

But she did, with flair, for thirty-three years.

Then at the age of fifty-seven, it was over. To her amazement, her husband arrived home one day and told Dawn that he hated their life and wanted out. In Egypt, all a man needs to say to free himself from his wife is "I divorce you" three times, and it was nearly as easy for Dawn's husband to leave her.

The breakup blindsided Dawn, hitting her with the force of a natural disaster. She'd planned her future as half of a couple and had never dreamed she could be so swiftly catapulted into the ranks of older divorced mothers. In a single day, the plot of her life drastically changed.

Her husband distanced himself not only from her, but also from their two children, who were devastated by his departure. He left them all no money, and when he proposed that they sell their beloved beach house, Dawn decided to move there herself.

In the months that followed, I heard her continuing tales of financial hardship and sadness. It was clear she had to make a choice—whether to nurse her wounds and continue with the marginal income her nonprofit job provided or throw herself into her own self-preservation.

Her children helped her decide; she needed to be strong for them. She faced the fact that no one else was going to save her, so she went about saving herself. Quitting her nonprofit position, she found a spot in a highly competitive financial services business, a new field that she had to learn from the ground up. She funneled her organized, persuasive energy into this new position. Pushing herself, she discovered strengths and skills that had been buried under the rubble of her divorce and actually found herself flourishing in this new environment.

Dawn buckled down, rented her house out during peak summer months, and counted her pennies. Eventually she worked her way out of debt and was able to buy her former husband's share of the beach house. In five short years in her new industry, she pulled off the biggest deal in her field, becoming a kind of modern day Scarlett O'Hara, saving the family home from divorce and debt.

It took a major setback for Dawn to realize that she is more than capable of taking care of her own financial security. She overcame the setback of her divorce by taking control of her earning power and by rallying all of her inherent resources. Just like Dawn, women are capable of supporting themselves and their children. But it takes confidence and a belief that you have something to offer the world.

Of course, Dawn lives in a place where, with hard work and determination, financial transformation is possible. Women in other parts of the world are often limited by social and cultural barriers.

In India, Suame Singh runs a domestic violence/micro-enterprise program in a city about an hour's plane ride west of New Delhi. She met with me in New York to learn about Count Me In and about possible markets for her gorgeous silk products in the United States.

Toward the end of our meeting her interpreter told me

that when she was nineteen, her husband tried to kill her by soaking her in kerosene. Luckily, her neighbor rescued her before he could light the match. Even then, it took her five years to get a divorce. Her response? She decided to start and grow a program that teaches women who have been abused by their families how to read and write and make a living. Suame used her personal setback as a catalyst to help other women in her position. And she knew that women's ability to support themselves financially— "make a living" is such an appropriate phrase—was the key to remaking their lives.

The thing about setbacks large or small is that we can learn the most from them. They'll only hold you back if you let them. Imagine if we'd ditched the idea of Take Our Daughters to Work Day after the first twinge of doubt. Imagine if the women of Make Mine a Million $ Business folded their companies after a bad quarterly report. Imagine what you will miss in your life if you let lack of confidence or money hold you back. Use the tools and exercises outlined in this chapter and move to the next chapter to find a supportive group of people—your community who will help you grow and encourage you to have it your way.

6

ACTIVATE WHO YOU KNOW

Election Day and the day after were like holidays when I was growing up. My parents got up very early to help open the polling place at the local school and my father would then spend the day rounding up votes for himself or other candidates. As a family we would go to the election night celebrations staying up way too late to go to school the next day. It was clear to me that my father's success depended on family, friends, neighbors, colleagues, and constituents— a community—turning out to vote for and support him. In exchange he represented their interests by increasing jobs, equality, and protecting the environment. As Joe Merlino's power and influence increased, his community expanded from the town he represented as city attorney of Trenton, to the multiple counties he represented as a member of the state legislature, to the entire State of New Jersey as the Senate president. My father never would have been able to bring his vision to life for his family or state without his community.

Think about the vision you are developing of life, love, and work your way. You've activated your imagination and hopefully are getting clearer on exactly what you are best at so that your confidence is up. Now turn your attention to the people part: Who are the people in your life, in your community, who will help you achieve your dreams? And what will you do for them in exchange?

Community is an essential element of a good life. It involves sharing common purpose and goals and seeing each member as an important contributor. Community can be based on a physical place like a neighborhood, business, or school or it can be a group, even a virtual group, of people with common interests—single mothers, women farmers, mothers of twins, business owners, breast cancer survivors, political activists, widows. The message of this chapter is straightforward: you can be an independent person, capable of taking care of yourself and your family, but you will only get so far if you are trying to do it all by yourself.

Two, three, four brains figuring out a knotty problem are almost always better than one, and we benefit from hearing about other people's experiences with success and failure. We're inspired and guided by their stories. A strong community supports you, challenges you, and keeps you accountable. When you have questions or need support, you can ask for it.

Everyone Needs Help
Being independent does not mean doing everything yourself!

You Know More People than You Think

How did you meet your best friend? Your employer? Your significant other? Your mechanic? Your neighbor? Your babysitter? My guess is that you probably met most people in your life through other people in your life. As you know, I met my husband through my accountant. Connections happen all the time, every day, all around us. You won't even realize how many people you know—and who they know—until you activate your network.

Activating who you know means reaching out to the people in your personal and professional lives. It means sharing your goals with supportive people. It means asking others for advice, suggestions, connections, ideas, feedback, and more. That's how you grow a network.

For every campaign I have developed like Take Our Daughters to Work Day there was an advisory board that provided valuable support, feedback, and accountability. At Count Me In we have a wonderful board of directors that plays a pivotal role in guiding and growing the organization. I can remember the moment I met each member of my board because each and every one of them has helped me understand something new, meet someone I needed to meet, or solve a problem in a way I never would have imagined. Board members can connect you with their networks, which in turn expands your community and each board member's community.

Whether you are in business or not, it is key to have a board of advisors in mind that you call on and consult with as you construct life your way.

A good way to start constructing an informal board of advisors is with our best friend Google and her sisters Facebook, MySpace, and LinkedIn. With the Internet, we are all just a degree or two of separation from pretty much anyone. Even if you can't meet or talk to all of the people in person who can inspire or help you, you have the entire World Wide Web at your fingertips. You can peruse millions of people's profiles on Facebook or MySpace, join groups of like-minded people on Ning.com or other social networks, access advice and inspiration through blogs and discussion groups, and post questions and make professional connections on a professional networking site like LinkedIn.com.

Create Your Very Own Board of Advisors

Who do you know or who would you like to know who would sign on to be part of your informal advisory board? Think about people who want to see you succeed, who know things you don't, and who will respond to very specific, well-thought-out plans and questions from you.

Tools to Activate Who You Know

From my background in politics and running large-scale campaigns, I know a few things about networking. It's been exciting to share and practice all of my networking skills with the women of the Make Mine a Million $ Business community. First, let's look at the tools that have helped them and helped me to activate who we know, and then I'll share some examples of how we have used our networks to succeed.

1. Start with One Name

When you are really struggling with something, rather than getting caught up in how you are going to figure it out, you instead need to think about who you know who can help you. There is almost always someone you know who can lead you to the next step—someone you've met at a job, at a party, in high school, college, friends of your parents, doctors, whomever. Start with one willing person. Be clear with them what you want to do and how they can help you.

When I was working in presidential campaigns in the 1980s, before everyone had a computer, I worked with a telephone and a single legal pad on my desk. Generally, we received one name in the city where we were planning an event, and from that one name I would build an entire event.

Here's how it worked: I would call that one person and tell him or her that I was part of a campaign and new to the city. I explained what we wanted to do and asked for some advice. Then, after receiving that person's advice and ideas, I'd ask if he or she could connect me to someone else who could be helpful. Then I would do this again and again and again, until I had pages of names, phone numbers, ideas, and new connections. Some people wouldn't be very helpful, but as long as I got another contact to pursue, I was able to keep moving. Most people were happy to help if I was genuine in my request, clear about what I wanted, grateful for any assistance and quick to offer to return the favor.

It's like the detectives on *Law & Order* who visit a crime scene and come away with one lead—an eyewitness, a fingerprint, an unmarked key, a gun, anything. Then they follow that one lead until it leads to another lead and another and the crime is ultimately solved.

2. Periodically Review

Review your address book, contact database, PDA, cell phone, or wherever you keep your contacts on a regular basis.

Most people look through their address book once a year when they send holiday cards. Or they update their contact list when they are looking for a new job or making an invitation list for their one-year-old's birthday party. If you are serious about living your best life, then you need to review your contacts much more frequently—once a month at least.

By reviewing your contacts you get a spark of an idea. You don't know what your community can offer until you activate it, even just by flipping pages of a dog-eared address book.

3. How to Exchange Favors

Luckily for me, exchanging favors has always been a part of my life. Growing up in politics, I observed a constant exchange of conversations, favors, and phone calls. It was just understood that you would be there to help someone and they would be there to help you. I have built organizations and campaigns because people like my ideas and share my vision, but also because I help people and ask for help in return.

This is a very important issue for women—we have to get comfortable with the circle of giving and getting. I don't think you get very far if you aren't in the giving and getting business. People love helping other people, and people often need help. It's all a circle. If you're only taking or only giving, you are not keeping the circle in motion.

Here is all you have to say: "I respect your opinion and want to get your thoughts about my idea/opportunity/job/product." Be very clear and specific about what you want from the person.

Every person has value and we are all needed and in need at various points in our lives. Trust that it's okay to "pay it forward." Also know that you are never obligated to do anything that you feel is unethical or uncomfortable. You can always say no to a networking request that doesn't feel right.

EXERCISE: Build Your Favor Muscle

Do you feel uncomfortable with networking? Try this exercise to build your networking muscle and get more comfortable with asking for favors and doing favors.

Think about someplace you want to get to—such as finding an acting class, creating a new Web site for your business, or joining an organic food co-op—and this week ask for three favors from three different people, perhaps a phone number or a piece of advice, anything you need to move closer to your goal. You have to start asking for things. This is just like building a muscle; you have to practice. Make a mental note of who was helpful. Ask if there is anything you can do for them.

4. Give the Support You Want to Receive

Margery Miller, in her departing message to the Make Mine a Million $ Business community, shared the following advice that encapsulates not only activating who you know, but also making sure to pass your knowledge on to others. Her message resonated with this particular community, because one of our main goals is to provide women with a large network of support to help their businesses grow:

Learn from each other. Don't think you can do this by yourself! This is a unique opportunity to be in daily contact with some of the smartest women on the planet—all of you! You all have something to contribute to the growth of one another's businesses. You are the vanguard group of women business owners who can inspire, lead, and encourage other women to do what you are doing, and more! As I built my sales organization through the seventies, eighties, and nineties, I had very few people around me that had a clue about what my actual problems and issues were. At this moment, there are hundreds of you who can be resources for each other. Contribute to the group, ask for help from your peers, tell others about your successes. You are making a difference in the world, and we all benefit from your experiences.

One of the best ways to activate who you know is to generously share what you know. Asking "What can I do to help you?" is a great way to build a connection with someone. It's amazing how many women who teach workshops to the Make Mine a Million $ Business community say that they feel they gain more from teaching than their students do!

Meet the Community of Make Mine a Million $ Business

At our very first Make Mine a Million $ Business event in Washington, D.C., over fifty women business owners visited Capitol Hill to meet with members of Congress. That visit was about growing their businesses and professional networks, but there was a bigger picture: that growing women-owned businesses to million-dollar enterprises is about women creating their own success while they are creating jobs for millions of people (including some of their proud husbands), growing the American economy, and keeping our country innovative and competitive in the global market.

In fact, we have been so inspired by the women who have reached the million-dollar mark after joining the Make Mine a Million $ Business community that we decided to create a "race" for more women to grow their businesses. Just like the walk/run marathons you or your friends may have done to benefit breast cancer research or other causes, women participating in this race can choose their pace according to what kind of shape their business is in. "Runners" are racing toward the million-dollar mark, while "walkers" can set their sights on reaching $250,000 or $500,000 by December 31, 2009. (Learn more about the race at www.countmein.org.)

The race offers women entrepreneurs an online social network and educational resources that allow them to tap into the support and wisdom of women who have already run down this road. (For more on the Race to a Million,

visit www.makemineamillion.org.) Two of the women inspiring the racers are Make Mine a Million $ Business
awardees Gina Stern and Linda Russell. As you will see in
their stories, community is one of the major factors that
helped Gina and Linda step out of line and achieve all
that they are capable of.

Transforming the Airport Experience

Gina Stern is now a Make Mine a Million $ Business
awardee, but she grew up Puerto Rican in the Bronx
where, in her words, everyone ended up on drugs, pregnant, or dead. Late one day for high school after a brutal
fight at home, an unkind teacher told Gina to stop wasting
her time and to drop out of school. So she did.

But she had the confidence in herself to believe that
failure wasn't her destiny. Even with a dysfunctional,
drug-ridden family and no support network, she found a
way to step out of her line in the Bronx and get back into
school, where she found people who would support her.
She got a degree in fashion design. In the late 1990s, she
had a brainstorm: why not have luxurious spas in airports?
Given all of the waiting people do in airports, why not give
them a place to go where they can get great services and
relax from the stressful airport environment? So Gina
started a business, departure spas (www.departurespa.
com).

"It took me almost two years to get into my first airport,"

she says. "I didn't know anything about the beauty business. I was pitching to an airport used to having established, international brand retailers. I hadn't run any business, but I had a good idea and passion. Even though I wasn't a national brand and had no track record, for some reason I didn't see those as limitations."

Gina opened three spas—two in Newark Airport and one in Orlando. She survived the impact of 9/11 on the travel business and built her business close to $1 million in revenue. Than her landlord in Newark tried to push her out in favor of a chain of nail salons. Gina felt like another kind of teacher was showing up to tell her to drop out, to quit. Around that same time, a friend heard an ad for Make Mine a Million $ Business on the radio and told her about it. Gina says her mind shifted when she first visited the Web site and found answers to many of the questions she had been afraid to ask:

> When I won the award package from Make Mine a Million $ Business, the first thing was I got help and I got answers. Before that, I was afraid to ask people for help because I was afraid they would see me as not knowing what I was doing. When everyone thinks you're great but you have problems you can't own your success.
>
> Once I was part of a bigger program, I got knowledge and answers. When you start to struggle in your business you lose your vision a little bit. It bends. You start questioning yourself. And other

people have networks in place and systems, but I don't have that.

Someone who comes from where I come from rarely has a network like Make Mine a Million $ Business provides. They take you in and make you feel safe. And by winning an award package sponsored by major corporations, it meant something that big companies endorsed what I was doing. That made me feel respected.

Recently I was invited to speak at Union High School in Union, New Jersey, to a group of at-risk youth. It was the most amazing experience. Now I feel successful because I was able to go back. I was looking in their eyes and knowing that was exactly where I was supposed to be.

Instead of ending up on drugs, pregnant, or dead, Gina Stern is now running a successful business and helping inner-city girls see that the same future is possible for them. If Gina can do it, they can too.

Gina's story exemplifies the power of activating your network. Despite major challenges and setbacks, Gina kept turning to people—teachers, friends, and now Make Mine a Million $ Business community members and sponsors—for support, advice, and confidence. I have no doubt that the work she is doing to help high school girls will help her build an even stronger network and a more fulfilling and successful life.

Transforming School Photos

Linda Russell is another Make Mine a Million $ Business awardee who has stepped out of line and defined success on her own terms. The daughter of an unhappy single mother, Linda found herself in an unhappy marriage with an abusive, drug-addicted husband and two young children.

"For a few years it was just a nightmare," she says. "Eventually I had to go from denial to reality. One day he just went nuts, and I grabbed the kids and I went into a shelter. Six months before, when I started to realize that I was going to be a single mother, I'd sat down with a neighbor who was an accountant. I thought I'd have to go get a job at the supermarket. She said, 'Why don't you become a photographer? You love taking pictures and you have the camera, the equipment, the talent.' Once I hooked into that energy, grace stepped in. It all started to happen."

By activating who she knew—a supportive neighbor with accounting expertise—Linda was able to activate what she knew—photography—to change her life. Slowly but surely, Linda built a photography business, Mugshots Photography (www.mugshotsphotography.com).

At the beginning, she ran the business from her public housing apartment. Today, she owns her own home in Marin County, California, and her goal now is nothing short of revolutionizing school photography by taking creative photos, rather than the same-old blue-background boring shots that have been around forever. Another aspect of Linda's goal is to build a community of photographers who agree with her philosophy of photographing kids. Like Gina Stern, one of the lessons she's learned from the Make Mine a Million $ Business community is how important it is to expand your vision of success to include others.

Speaking of kids, Linda is a successful mom, too. Amazingly, Linda's daughter Jesse graduated from high school just one day before she received the Make Mine a Million $ Business award package.

"I am really no longer a functioning victim," Linda says. "I am a victor."

As a side note, I have to tell you that I learned one of the best lessons from Linda. I should probably save this for the end of the book, because it's probably what you'll remember, but I can't wait. Linda taught me how to pose for a picture so I don't look like I have four chins. Here is the tip: Your chin needs to always be in front of your chest. Lean into the camera like you're shaking hands. Heavier people tend to believe they should back away from the camera to look smaller, but what you're actually doing is spreading your chest—this gives you more chins and makes you look even more round! So put that chin forward and lean into the photo. You'll have pictures of yourself that you will want to keep.

208 / Nell Merlino

The World Is Your Network

Gina Stern and Linda Russell are examples of asking for help and receiving it, even in very challenging life situations. They are also examples of giving back every bit of what they received from other people. The thing about activating your network is that you never know where your connections can take you. So explore every relationship that feels right and involve as many people as you'd like in your efforts to create the most fulfilling, joyful life you can. Community is crucial.

Your community is a circle and, of course, our planet is a circle. Ultimately, everything connects. In the final chapter, we'll bring the stories of Take Our Daughters to Work Day and Make Mine a Million $ Business full circle. As you'll see, there is an undeniable connection between the lives we lead as girls and the lives we lead as women. We learn and grow as girls from watching those in our communities, and girls learn and grow by watching us.

7

GIRLS LEARN EVERYTHING
FROM WATCHING US

On the morning of the very first Take Our Daughters to Work Day, a little girl and her father walked into a bustling blue-collar coffee shop in downtown Brooklyn. It was one of those old places, positioned right next to a busy subway stop, that hasn't changed in sixty years, with linoleum flooring and a row of worn-in stools at the counter. The little girl, all dressed up, sat on a stool beside her father and the other working-class guys. She ordered a hot chocolate from the waitress.

The waitress leaned over and asked where the girl was going. She explained that she was going to work with her dad. Her father then told the waitress it was Take Our Daughters to Work Day. The girl explained further, "My teacher told us the day was all about where girls get their steam."

The girl mixed up "steam" with "self-esteem," and I love that she did that.

Take Our Daughters to Work Day was designed for exactly what she described—to give girls the "steam" to come out of the private, hidden space of the home and into workplaces in public. We wanted girls to be where the action is. Once they saw it, they could better imagine themselves in it.

There is scientific proof of this. For example, according to Lovann Brizendine in *The Female Brain,* from the time they are born, baby girls mimic faces at four hundred times the rate of boys. If you have a daughter, niece, or granddaughter, this fact won't surprise you at all. My two-year-old niece Helena is a prime example. If I am wearing a ponytail, she wants to wear a ponytail. If I say "meow!" then she says "meow!" When I say "cucumber," then she says "umber." As she grows older, if I say "I can't," or "I'm too fat" or "I'm not good enough," then she might, too.

Whatever world we want for our daughters, we have to start to claim for ourselves. So many women say that they want their daughters to have what women don't have today. That is just another way of waiting in line. We have to step out of line and stop waiting right now—for ourselves and because our daughters and all little girls are watching. Girls learn everything from watching us.

President Bill Clinton, himself the father of a daughter, captured the vital importance of raising strong girls in a message he shared on the occasion of the second Take Our Daughters to Work Day:

> This event offers an important reminder that women make invaluable contributions in every aspect of national life. As we look to the horizon of the twenty-

first century, our young women must realize that America's success depends on their confidence, their creativity, and their dreams. Take Our Daughters to Work Day is only a day in the lives of all those participating, but the lessons learned today can have lasting impact on this next generation of leaders. Today, we pause to show our daughters how much we value them. Every day, we must teach them that if they value themselves enough, they can change the world.

That message is not just for girls. It's for all of us. If we value ourselves enough, we can lead personally fulfilling lives, and, in the process, change the opportunities available for ourselves and other women and girls. Forever.

We Are All Daughters

Whenever I did media interviews for Take Our Daughters to Work Day, reporters always asked me how old my daughter was. "I didn't have a daughter when I imagined Take Our Daughters to Work Day," I would tell them (by the first event I had my wonderful stepdaughter, Laura). "This is about my being one."

I've written quite a bit in this book about my parents, Joe and Molly Merlino, because they have each had such a profound influence on me. You may feel this way about one or both of your parents, and your children will likely feel this way about you.

Sometimes you don't even realize the effects your parents have had. In my case, it was pretty obvious. Although I no longer work in politics like my father did, I have always known that public service is my calling. And I remember the first time I became aware of what it meant to live a life of public service. It was the day my father was sworn in as assistant prosecutor. I was five or six years old and I knew it was an important day because someone had sent a huge bouquet of flowers to our house and we didn't have to go to school. All of the kids were dressed in our best clothes and the girls had to wear white gloves, even though it wasn't Sunday. I liked it.

I knew instinctively that my father was going to be doing an important job. All of the adults were saying that he was a great guy. And he had to take an oath—he had to swear on a Bible to a man in a long robe—to do his job well. That meant something huge to me. I wanted that important responsibility. I wanted people to trust me to help them and stand up with them. And I knew it was possible to do that with my life because I saw my own father doing it.

EXERCISE: What Did You See?

What did you see as a girl? Who did you admire and want to grow up to be like?

Who did you not admire as a girl? Who did you want to grow up and not be like?

What action can you take in your life right now to be more like the people you admired as a girl?

What Do You Want Your Daughter to See?

When Anucha Browne Sanders filed a harassment suit against Isiah Thomas, she said that she thought of her thirteen-year-old daughter who will one day enter the workforce. When Charlene Foster stepped through her fears and gave her Make Mine a Million $ Business presentation, she did it to be a role model for her kids. I created Take Our Daughters to Work Day so that every girl could have the same life-changing moment I had when I saw my parents happy and fulfilled at work.

What can you do for your children? What do you want every girl to know is possible? What do you want your daughter or other girls never to see or feel? It is up to you—to us—to decide what the world will look like for girls and what they will believe is possible. We make choices every day and girls are watching our every move. It is another great reason to step out of line and live the life you want. By doing so, you will show another girl another path that is possible for her, too.

EXERCISE: What Do You Desire for Your Daughter (and All Young Girls in the World)?

What changes do you hope our daughters will see in their lifetime?

What are the obstacles you've overcome that you hope your daughter won't have to face?

What can you do to be a positive role model for a girl today?

To Be for Our Daughters, We Must Be for Ourselves

In bathrooms, boardrooms, buses, bagel shops, and everywhere else, we all need to imagine that there is a little girl following us around, repeating everything we say and everything we do. Think about all the things you want for yourself and your daughters and granddaughters and little girls everywhere—and teach them by living it yourself.

What does this mean? We must step out of lines we don't want our daughters to wait in. We can't say one thing and do another. We can't tell a girl that she can achieve anything she wants and then not be engaged and learning about things ourselves. Let's not settle for an unfulfilling life and then tell a girl to pursue her dreams. Perfection is not required; we just need to live life on our own terms so girls can learn to live life on their own terms, too.

Margery Miller calls this being "wisely selfish." She says, "The greatest thing you can do for all those around you is take excellent care of yourself and live your life with integrity. You are a role model for everyone who comes in contact with you. So ask yourself, what are you doing today that nurtures you, nourishes you, fills you up? How much time do you spend on self-care? If you are dragging by the end of the day, that means that your work and your life are draining you, not energizing you. We are born to serve, we are here to serve, but if we leave ourselves out of the equation then everyone suffers, especially you!"

Be Wisely Selfish

If you want to serve others, you must take care of yourself first. Do things every single day that nurture you, fill you up, and make you happy. You'll benefit yourself and the people around you.

My Mother, My Hero

During the writing of this book, I received an e-mail from a Make Mine a Million $ Business awardee named

Robin Moorad, whose business, Imago Associates (www. imagoassociates.com), has reached and surpassed the million-dollar mark. She forwarded an essay to me that had been written by her fourteen-year-old daughter as a class assignment to write about one of her heroes. Here is an excerpt from the essay:

> Robin Moorad wakes up every Sunday morning to watch her favorite show, *CBS Sunday Morning*. After a long week of work, she sits on the sofa with her loving dogs, Mochi and Buddy, at her feet. Her soft footsteps are careful not to wake me (her daughter) in the nearby room. She relaxes in the morning only to work in the afternoon. Working at home, she does a great job of separating her work life from her personal life with me. The mere fact that she has started a business on her own and was fearless in doing so is a great inspiration to me. However, it is not just the big things that make her my hero, but the small gestures.
>
> Robin does her best to separate her work life from her personal life with me. Her work stops after she leaves the office and isn't brought out to our common areas. A person can only have one life, but she makes it seem possible to be two different people. Sometimes I'll be sitting in the car with her when she receives a business call; she'll pick up the phone and her posture and voice change, even her laugh. Her personalities make it possible to have a

normal home life; they make me feel comfortable and safe, so that we have some privacy as a family.

I know that when I wake up in the morning, there will be breakfast on the table, quarters in her wallet for the bus, even the car pulled out of the driveway waiting for me. I know that when she tells me to wash my own clothes, make my own food, or sometimes to feed and walk the dogs, she is only trying to prepare me for later in life. I ask her what motivates her to do better, she says, "I guess I'm just wired that way." Well, my motivation is to be just like her: live a balanced life, do what you like, and do not be afraid to try new things and go on an adventure. I want to be someone's hero just like she is for me.

When Robin Moorad starts her own business and succeeds, her daughter succeeds too. When women act on their own behalf and live the lives we want, girls do too. When you act on your own behalf, girls will see you and believe they can be anything they want to be. To support this notion, Count Me In has launched a new program called Make Our Daughters a Million, which provides inspiration and support for girls to think entrepreneurially. Girls learn everything from watching us.

The Time Is Now

When you make the choice to step out of line and live the life you want—with your money, your confidence, your family, your spirituality, your health, your relationships, your work—you are forging a new path for all women. We all can grow and succeed when you empower yourself to find a loving relationship with "the right kind of fella" or gal on Match.com. We all grow and succeed when women in Rwanda take control of parliament and sort out what to do with half a million orphans. We'd all grow and succeed if we spent our time in a ladies' room line learning about girls in Liberia and helping them gain access to water and education. When you stop waiting for your life to change, step out of line, and step into your power, you change our world.

Whenever you feel stuck or need an extra boost of confidence on your journey, think back to some of the main lessons in this book.

Use your imagination. Every time you're struggling with a challenge, start by using your imagination to envision the best outcome you can. Until you have some vision of where you're going, you can't figure out how to get there. You can have the life you want as soon as you can see it first.

Bust the savior fantasy. It is perfectly fine if your vision of your best life looks nothing like your current life. However, it is not okay if your vision looks like a fairy tale. Bust the savior fantasy and get real. You are your own savior.

Trust that the system is more malleable than you think. Don't worry about the way things have always been done. The truth is that systems change all the time to suit our needs. Families morph. Structures shift. Bureaucracies jiggle and rattle and shake. Once you look more closely at the systems holding you back in your life, you'll see that they are malleable, too.

Find like-minded supporters. Whatever it is you want in your life, start talking about it. Tell people. Share. Google. Slowly but surely, you will begin to find your way. Inevitably, other people will hear something in your idea that resonates with their lives and they will want to be part of your efforts. That is exactly what happened with Take Our Daughters to Work Day and Make Mine a Million $ Business, and that is what can happen for you.

Gain from complaining. If you're not exactly sure what you want your life to look like, try thinking about the things that make you mad. What bothers you so much that you really want to change it? What problems or frustrations do you want to solve? What drives you crazy? Deep passion—positive or negative—provides clues to what life path you will find fulfilling.

Be more like Dora. Take a confidence lesson from a little girl. Get rid of any lingering images of what women, mothers, daughters, sisters, wives, girlfriends, or super-heroes should be, and live more like Dora the Explorer—explore your own bravery and definitions of success.

Overcome setbacks large and small. You always have a choice how you deal with adversity. Make the conscious choice to thrive. Setbacks can be the greatest catalysts for success if you acknowledge their lessons and then keep putting one foot in front of the other to achieve your ultimate goals.

Activate who you know. You can't do everything yourself and you don't have to. The world is your network, so start with the people you know and keep building your support system from there. The more support you give, the more you will receive. Community makes everything possible, and it makes your achievements more meaningful—and fun.

Act with the knowledge that girls learn everything from watching us. Whatever world we want for our daughters, we have to start to claim for ourselves.

Finally, imagine if, instead of hoping to be discovered like Lana Turner or Kate Moss, every woman woke up in the morning and said to herself: "I'm going to discover myself today." How would all of our lives change?

My answer: Let's try it and find out!

Final Thoughts: Living Outside the Lines

Think back to that woman I saw that hot July day in the ladies' room line of a rest stop on the New York Thruway. She was looking back and forth, back and forth, but never moving from her spot in line. Now we know we can move anytime we want. Stepping out of line is up to us. We each have the power. We can find a relationship, make a difference in the world, have an enjoyable family life, grow a business, like our jobs, love our bodies, or do anything else we want. And every time we do something to help ourselves, the world becomes bigger and better for all women.

As I write these final words, the U.S. economy is in a downward spiral and many jobs are being lost. I, for one, am optimistic. When I think of the 10.5 million women-owned businesses in the country, I imagine that one million of them will grow this year to produce just one new job each. In one swoop, women will have replaced a million lost jobs in this country! In less than twenty years, I will have gone from working on a program that made young girls more visible by taking them into the workplace to a program that could help women put a million Americans back to work. That's incredible!

Maybe it all boils down to physics. Every time we make a positive change for one woman, the change has an effect on every man, woman, and child around her. If you change how you do things, everything will change. Whatever you want in life, step out of line and go get it right now. And then share it with the world. Girls will be watching and the effects will last forever.

About the Author

NELL MERLINO is founder, president, and CEO of Count Me In for Women's Economic Independence, the leading national not-for-profit provider of resources for women to grow their micro businesses into million $ enterprises through its signature program, Make Mine a Million $ Business.® Throughout her career, Nell Merlino has been inspiring millions of people to take action. She is the creative force behind Take Our Daughters to Work Day, which moved more than 71 million Americans to participate in a day dedicated to giving girls the opportunity to dream bigger about their futures. Merlino has worked on campaigns for the YWCA, The Week Without Violence, the United Nations' Fourth World Conference on Women in Beijing, and in two state governments. She was an advance woman in presidential campaigns, a union organizer, and a Fulbright Scholar, and has received numerous awards, including the Fulbright Award for Outstanding Achievement, the Forbes Trailblazer Award, and the Matrix Award for Achievement in Communications. Merlino lives in Manhattan with her husband, Gary Conger.